E. M. Forster's

# A Passage to India

*adapted for the stage by*

**Martin Sherman**

**Methuen Drama**

*for Nancy Meckler*

*A Passage to India* premiered at the Richmond Theatre, Surrey, on 18 September 2002. The cast was as follows:

| | |
|---|---|
| **Dr Aziz** | Paul Bazeley |
| **Adela Quested** | Penny Laden |
| **Mahmoud Ali** } **Tiger** | Nicholas Khan |
| **Cyril Fielding** | Ian Gelder |
| **Miss Derek** } **Mrs Turton** | Priyanga Elan |
| **Mrs Moore** | Susan Engel |
| **Professor Narayan** **Godbole** } **Burton** | Aaron Neil |
| **Turton** } **McBryde** | Geoffrey Beevers |
| **Ronny Heaslop** } **Ralph** | Guy Lankester |
| **Rafi/Das** | Daniel Hope |
| **Hamidullah** | Antony Bunsee |

*Director* Nancy Meckler
*Designer* Niki Turner
*Lighting Designer* Chris Davey
*Composer* Peter Salem

*A Passage to India* was commissioned by Shared Experience, a company that unites both physical and text-based theatre, creating an individual and distinctive performance style. This meant I could dare to imagine the most complicated and sometimes spectacular scenes in the knowledge that the director, Nancy Meckler, would translate them into a visual language at once simple and evocative. Thus the stage directions in this text are not to be taken literally, but instead as a blueprint for a passage into theatrical possibility.

# A Passage to India

**Martin Sherman** was born in Philadelphia, educated at Boston University and now lives in London. His plays include: *Passing By, Cracks* and *Rio Grande* (Playwrights Horizons, New York); *Bent* (Royal Court Theatre, London, 1979, subsequently West End and Broadway, where it received a Tony nomination for Best Play and won the Dramatist's Guild Hull-Warriner award). *Bent* has been performed in over thirty-five countries and was revived by the National Theatre in 1989. His other plays include *Messiah* (Hampstead Theatre and Aldwych, London, 1983); *When She Danced* (King's Head Theatre, London, 1988 and Gielgud, 1991); *A Madhouse in Goa* (Lyric Hammersmith and Apollo Theatre, London, 1989); *Some Sunny Day* (Hampstead Theatre, 1996); *Rose* (National Theatre, London, 1999) which received a Olivier nomination for Best Play and transferred to Broadway in 2000. His screenplays include: *The Clothes in the Wardrobe* (BBC Television, 1992; US title *The Summer House*, 1994); *Alive and Kicking; Bent* (1997); Franco Zefferelli's *Callas Forever* and *The Roman Spring of Mrs Stone*.

Published by Methuen 2002

3 5 7 9 10 8 6 4 2

First published in 2002 by
Methuen Publishing Limited
215 Vauxhall Bridge Road,
London SW1V 1EJ

Methuen Publishing Limited Reg. No. 3543167

ISBN 0 413 77289 6

Typeset by SX Composing DTP, Rayleigh, Essex
Printed and bound in Great Britain by
Cox & Wyman Ltd, Reading, Berkshire

# Act One

**Professor Narayan Godbole** *addresses the audience. He is sitting on strip of carpet. He is barefoot and in white. He wears a pale-blue turban.*

**Godbole**   Long before Dr Aziz settled in our state, in Mau, another young Mohammedan lived here.

*A beautiful* **Young Man** *stands in a ray of light. He is naked except for a loincloth. He is in front of a house. An older woman – his* **Mother** *– comes out of the house. She looks at him sternly.*

**Godbole**   One day his mother said to him – free the prisoners. So he took a sword and went up to the fort. He unlocked a door and the prisoners streamed out and resumed their former occupations, but the police were too much annoyed and cut off the young man's head.

*The* **Young Man**, *the* **Prisoners**, *the* **Police** *act out the story as* **Godbole** *relates it.*

**Godbole**   Ignoring its absence he made his way over the rocks that separated the fort and the town, killing policemen as he went, and fell outside his mother's house.

*The* **Young Man** *stretches the sword out to his* **Mother** *and dies.*

**Godbole**   Consequently, there are two shrines to that young man today, here in our town – that of the Head above, and that of the Body below . . .

**Villagers** *turn the* **Young Man**'*s body and then his head into two separate shrines, which stand on either side of the stage for the rest of the play.*

**Godbole**   . . . and although ours is a Hindu state, they are worshipped by all who live here. The Shrine of the Body actually lies in Dr Aziz's garden. The Shrine of the Head is a short walk down. He takes his children there sometimes. Shall I tell you about Dr Aziz?

*Pause.*

Actually, the young man – he of the head and the body – is a saint, not a god. God is not born yet. Well, He will be, tonight, in our yearly festival. He has also been born centuries ago, nor can He ever be born, because He is the Lord of the Universe, who transcends human processes. He is, was not, is not, was. He stands with me now.

*He rises and stands on the carpet. he begins to sing.*

Radhakrishna, Radhkrishna,
Radhakrishna, Radhkrishna,
Krisnanradha, Krisnanradha,
Radhakrishna, Radhkrishna . . .

*He plays a cymbal. Inscriptions appear on banners. One of them reads* GOD SI LOVE. **Godbole** *looks up at the banner.*

Not everyone here can spell. And yet. God Si Love. Is that the final message of India? (*Pause.*) Who was I telling you about? Dr Aziz. Yes. Although he is a follower of Islam, he has settled here with his children – two years now. Dr Aziz came to us from Chandrapore. As did I. (*Pause.*) I am flooded with memories now, but they are meaningless. I think of an old woman I met in Chandrapore. Shall I tell you about her? Memories occur. I cannot stop them. I remember a wasp. Where did I see it? Perhaps on a stone. The stone and the wasp – and the old woman – I love equally. For I imitate God.

**Godbole**'s **Students** – *a* **Choir** – *appear by the side of the carpet. They sing along with him.*

**Godbole** *and* **Choir**

Radhakrishna Radhakrishna,
Radhakrishna Radhakrishna . . .

*The music intensifies. There is noise now. Distant thunder. Cymbals clashing. And incense.* **Godbole** *begins to dance on the carpet.*

*Suddenly* **Dr Aziz** *appears. He is handsome, compact, wiry, volatile.*

**Godbole** *stops.*

**Godbole**    Ah. Dr Aziz. We practise.

**Aziz**    Practise?

**Godbole**    Rehearse. For tonight's ceremony – the birth of our God. It is the main event of our religious year. And within it I rediscover my spirit. Well. You are perhaps waiting to greet our guest.

**Aziz**    Guest?

**Godbole**    He has arrived at the European guest house perhaps – at least possibly.

**Aziz**    Who?

**Godbole**    Did I not tell you? My former superior from Chandrapore.

**Aziz**    Fielding?

**Godbole**    He is on an inspection tour of Central India. He is with his wife and her brother. Surely I mentioned it.

**Aziz**    I have no desire to see Fielding. Or his wife.

**Aziz** *walks off.*

**Godbole** *returns to the audience, as if the interruption had not occurred.*

**Godbole**    I saw the old woman once again. The wasp as well. Now I leave. (*Pause.*) One old Englishwoman and one little wasp. It does not seem much; still, it is more than I am myself.

**Godbole** *leaves.*

**Aziz** *sits by the Shrine of the Body. He looks at the sky. Distant thunder. Suddenly two* **Climbers** *enter, or rather, run on pursued by bees. They are* **Fielding**, *an untidy, greying man – and a* **Boy**, *aged eighteen.* **Aziz** *is agitated by the sight of* **Fielding** *and starts to leave, but he is also amused by the bee attack. Finally he has to speak.*

**Aziz**    Hello, gentlemen, are you in trouble?

**Boy**   I've been stung.

**Aziz**   Lie down in a pool of water, my dear sir. Here are plenty. Don't come near me . . . I can't control them; they are State bees; complain to His Highness of their behaviour.

*The bees fly away.*

**Aziz**   They are gone now, at any rate. (*Goes to* **Boy**; *the* **Boy** *instinctively pulls away from him.*) Come, come – I am a doctor.

**Fielding** (*smiles*)   A very fine doctor.

**Aziz** *ignores him; the* **Boy** *gives* **Aziz** *his hand and* **Aziz** *pulls a couple of stings out of the* **Boy**'s *wrist.*

**Fielding**   How do you do, Aziz, after all this time? (**Aziz** *doesn't answer.*) How goes it, Aziz?

**Aziz**   In my usual health.

*Pause.*

**Fielding**   I have missed you, Aziz.

**Aziz** *stares at him, then turns away.*

**Aziz**   Do not trouble me here. That is all I ask. I do not want you.

**Fielding**   Aziz . . .

**Aziz**   I do not want any of you in my private life. I have forgotten all of you. You no longer exist.

*A mist envelops* **Aziz** *and the two* **Men**. *Mau disappears.*

*A* **Woman** (**Adela**) *appears in the mist, her face scratched, her clothes torn, her eyes dazed, and then she too disappears.*

*A mosque appears.*

*Chandrapore. Two years earlier.*

**Aziz** *walks into the mosque. A beautiful moonlit night. He sits on a low wall. He can hear sounds in the night – on the right, an amateur* *orchestra from the English club; elsewhere, Hindus drumming; somewhere else, mourners bewailing a corpse. An owl.*

*Suddenly there is movement. The mosque seems to quiver. An* **Englishwoman** *steps out into the moonlight, but her face is hidden.* **Aziz** *is angry.*

**Englishwoman**    Oh! Oh!

**Aziz**    Madame, this is a mosque, you have no right here at all; you should have taken off your shoes; this is a holy place for Moslems.

**Englishwoman**    I have taken them off.

**Aziz**    You have?

**Englishwoman**    I left them at the entrance.

**Aziz**    Then I ask your pardon.

*The* **Englishwoman**, *still startled, moves away.*

**Aziz**    I am truly sorry for speaking.

**Englishwoman**    Yes, I am right, was I not? If I remove my shoes I am allowed?

**Aziz**    Of course, but so few ladies take the trouble, especially if thinking no one is there to see you.

**Englishwoman**    That makes no difference. God is here.

**Aziz**    Madame!

**Englishwoman**    Please let me go.

**Aziz**    Can I do you some service – now or at any time?

**Englishwoman**    No, thank you, really none – goodnight.

**Aziz**    May I know your name?

**Englishwoman**    Mrs Moore.

*He moves towards her. She steps out of the shadows. We see that she is old; her voice deceived him.*

**Aziz**   Mrs Moore, I am afraid I startled you. I shall tell our community – my friends – about you. That God is here – very good, very fine indeed. I think that you are newly arrived in India.

**Mrs Moore**   Yes – how did you know?

**Aziz**   By the way you address me. Can I call you a carriage?

**Mrs Moore**   I have only come from the club. They are doing a play that I have seen in London and it was so hot . . .

**Aziz**   I think you ought not to walk at night alone, Mrs Moore. There are bad characters about and leopards may come across from the Marabar Hills. Snakes also.

**Mrs Moore**   But you walk about yourself.

**Aziz**   Oh, I am used to it.

**Mrs Moore**   Used to snakes?

**Aziz**   I'm a doctor. Snakes don't dare bite me.

*They laugh and sit down, side by side in the entrance, and slip on their evening shoes.*

May I ask you a question now? Why ever do you come to Chandrapore?

**Mrs Moore**   I have escorted a young lady here from England. She and my son contemplate marriage. But they are cautious. My son is the City Magistrate here.

**Aziz**   Oh no, excuse me, that is quite impossible. Our City Magistrate's name is Mr Heaslop.

**Mrs Moore**   He's my son all the same. I was married twice.

**Aziz**   Yes, now I see, and your first husband died.

**Mrs Moore**   He did, and so did my second husband.

**Aziz**    And is the City Magistrate the entire of your family now?

**Mrs Moore**    No, there are the young ones from my second marriage, Ralph and Stella, in England.

**Aziz**    Mrs Moore, this is all extremely strange, because like yourself, I have also two sons and a daughter. And their mother, my wife, has also died. We are in the same box.

**Mrs Moore**    And your children? . . .

**Aziz**    They are most comfortably with my wife's mother. I can see them whenever I like. They are such very, very small children.

**Mrs Moore**    What are their names? Not also Ronny, Ralph and Stella surely?

**Aziz**    No indeed. How funny it sounds. Their names are quite different and will surprise you. Listen, please. I am about to tell you my children's names. The first is called Ahmed, the second is called Karim, the third – she is the eldest – Jamila. Three children are enough. Do you not agree?

**Mrs Moore**    I do.

*They are both silent for a moment.*

**Aziz**    Would you care to see over the Lintel hospital one morning? I have nothing else to offer at Chandrapore.

**Mrs Moore**    Thank you, I have seen it already, or I should like to have come with you very much.

**Aziz**    I suppose my superior at the hospital, Major Callender, took you.

**Mrs Moore**    Yes, and Mrs Callender.

**Aziz**    Ah. A very charming lady.

**Mrs Moore**    Possibly, when one knows her better.

**Aziz**    What? What? You didn't like her?

**Mrs Moore**   She was certainly intending to be kind, but I did not find her exactly charming.

**Aziz**   Charming! She has just taken my tonga without my permission – do you call that being charming? And her husband, my superior at the hospital, interrupts me night after night from where I am dining with my friends, saying I must come to him at once, and I go at once, breaking up a most pleasant entertainment, and he is not there and not even a message, and then his wife runs past me, as I say, without even an acknowledgement, and takes my carriage. Is this charming? . . . Forgive me, my tongue runs ahead of my brain sometimes. My friends say I talk too much. But I think you understand me, you know what I feel. Oh, if others resembled you.

**Mrs Moore**   I don't think I do understand people very well. I only know whether I like – or dislike – them.

**Aziz**   Ah. (*Smiles.*) Then you are an Oriental.

*She smiles back.*

**Ronny Heaslop**'s *bungalow.* **Mrs Moore** *is knitting.* **Adela Quested** *bursts into the room. She is tremulous, in her late twenties.*

**Adela**   I want to see the *real* India.

**Mrs Moore**   I want to see it too and only wish we could. Apparently the Chief Administrator, Mr Turton, and his wife will arrange something for next Tuesday.

**Adela**   It'll end up in an elephant ride, it always does. I really didn't come up here to see *elephants*!

**Mrs Moore** (*amused*)   There are quite a few cows as well.

**Adela**   I thought I would go out of my mind this evening at the club. That dreadful play, *Cousin Kate.* I saw it last year in London with my play discussion group, and we had nothing to discuss – there were no *issues* involved. And then the meal after – sardines on toast, peas, cutlets, trifle, we might as well have been in Surrey. There were no spices. I

long for – yes, that's it – *flavour*! I was desperate to leave. As
indeed you seem to have done. Where were you off to? Did
you succeed in catching the moon in the Ganges?

**Mrs Moore**   I went to the mosque, but I did not catch the
moon.

**Ronny** *enters. He is in his early thirties.*

**Ronny**   Adela, have a drink? Mother, a drink?

**Mrs Moore**   No thank you, dear.

**Adela**   I was just saying, Ronny, that I'd like to see the
real India.

**Ronny**   Fielding says one can only see the real India by
seeing Indians. What a peculiar man he is.

**Mrs Moore**   Who is, dear?

**Ronny**   Fielding, the schoolmaster.

**Adela**   But excepting my own servant, whom I rather
distrust, I've scarcely spoken to an Indian since landing. Nor
have I seen anything other than the club. Your mother has
at least been to a mosque.

**Ronny**   Have you?

**Mrs Moore**   Yes, tonight.

**Ronny**   When?

**Mrs Moore**   Whilst the play was on.

**Ronny**   But Mother, you can't do that sort of thing.

**Mrs Moore**   Can't Mother?

**Ronny**   No, really not in this country. It's not done.
There's the danger from snakes for one thing.

**Mrs Moore**   Ah yes, so the young man there said.

**Adela**   This sounds very romantic. You met a young man
in a mosque and only now let me know? Was he nice?

**Mrs Moore**   Very nice.

**Ronny**   Who was he?

**Mrs Moore**   A doctor. I don't know his name.

**Ronny**   A doctor? I know of no young doctor in Chandrapore.

**Mrs Moore**   We had a lovely conversation. He told me about his children and then he walked me back to the club. He knows you.

**Ronny**   I wish you had pointed him out to me. I can't make out who he is.

**Mrs Moore**   He didn't come into the club. He said he wasn't allowed to.

**Ronny**   Oh, good gracious! Not a Mohammedan? Why ever didn't you tell me you'd been talking to a native.

**Adela**   A Mohammedan! How perfectly magnificent. Ronny, isn't that like your mother? While we talk about seeing the real India, she goes and sees it and then forgets she's seen it.

**Ronny**   What was he doing there himself at that time of night?

**Adela**   Perhaps it was prayer time.

**Ronny**   No, it's not their prayer time. You must tell me more about this native.

**Mrs Moore**   I believe he's connected to the hospital.

**Ronny**   Oh. Oh yes. Chap's name is Aziz. He's quite all right. Nothing against him at all.

**Mrs Moore**   Aziz! What a charming name!

**Ronny**   So you and he had a talk. Did you gather he was well-disposed? Did he seem to tolerate us – the brutal conqueror, that sort of thing?

**Mrs Moore**   Oh yes, I think so, except the Callenders – he doesn't care for the Callenders at all.

**Ronny**   Oh, so he told you that, did he? The Major will be interested.

**Mrs Moore**   Ronny, you're never going to pass it on to Major Callender!

**Ronny**   Yes, Mother, I must in fact.

**Mrs Moore**   But my dear boy – a private conversation!

**Ronny**   Nothing's private in India. Aziz knew that when he spoke out, so don't you worry. He had some motive in what he said.

**Mrs Moore**   You never used to judge people like this at home.

**Ronny**   India isn't home.

**Mrs Moore**   You really must not hand on to Major Callender anything I have told you about Dr Aziz.

**Adela**   No, Ronny, you mustn't. He sounds like a lovely chap. And your mother is quite right . . . a private conversation is sacrosanct.

**Ronny** (*smiles*)   Lovely word. But it doesn't apply out here. You are quite unaware of the social mores of this country.

**Adela**   I think not. I've read quite a lot about India. I've attended several lectures on the subject. I'm not uninformed.

**Ronny**   I didn't mean to suggest you were.

**Mrs Moore**   Adela, dear, might you fetch my playing cards?

**Adela**   Yes, what a good idea. There really doesn't seem to be any other way to pass the time.

**Adela** *leaves the room.*

**Ronny**   I do wish you would not talk about this Aziz
fellow to Adela.

**Mrs Moore**   Not talk about him. Why?

**Ronny**   I don't want Adela to be worried.

**Mrs Moore**   Why on earth should that worry her? At any
rate, she came out here to be worried. That's why she's
here. She discussed it all on the boat. She knows you in play,
as she put it, but not in work, and she felt she must come
and look around before she decides – and before you
decided. She is being very fair-minded.

**Ronny** (*dejected*)   I know.

**Mrs Moore**   But, dear, I did want to have this moment to
suggest that you ought to be more alone with her than you
are.

**Ronny**   Yes, perhaps, but then people'd talk.

**Mrs Moore**   Well, let them.

**Ronny**   It's difficult. People are odd out here. They notice
everything until they're perfectly sure that you're their sort.

**Mrs Moore**   I don't think Adela'll ever be quite their sort
– she's much too individual.

**Ronny**   I know, that's so remarkable about her. I suppose
nothing's on her mind?

**Mrs Moore**   Ask her yourself, my dear boy.

**Ronny**   But you can sense things.

**Mrs Moore**   Perhaps some of the people she's met at the
club are getting on her nerves; they make unpleasant
comments about the Indians, you see.

**Ronny**   How like a woman to worry over a side issue.
We're not here to make pleasant comments. Are we all
supposed to lose our ability to do good in this country
because our behaviour isn't always pleasant? I spend

my days in court trying to decide which of two untrue
accounts is less untrue, trying to protect the weak against the
less weak, indeed, trying to dispense justice and keep the
peace, and if along the way I or my associates are not
pleasant it is because we have something far more important
to do.

**Mrs Moore**    I disagree. The English *are* out here to be
pleasant.

**Ronny**    How do you make that out, Mother?

**Mrs Moore**    Because India is part of the earth. And God
has put us on earth in order to be pleasant to each other.
God . . . is . . . love.

**Ronny**    Yes. I quite see that. (*Pause.*) You must tell me if
you're feeling unwell.

**Mrs Moore**    Why is that?

**Ronny**    When you go all religious, it's often a symptom of
bad health.

**Mrs Moore** (*laughs*)    I should not have mentioned God.
I'm sorry. But He's difficult to avoid as one grows older.
He's been constantly in my thoughts since I entered this
country, though oddly enough, He satisfies me less. It's as
though there's an arch, and beyond that another arch, and
beyond that – silence. Do you understand?

*He stares at her. He doesn't.*

**Adela** *returns with playing cards.*

**Adela**    But Ronny, I was thinking, why *can't* we meet some
Indians? It's ridiculous to be in India and not to see Indians
– really, it's as simple as that.

**Mrs Moore** *shoots a knowing look at* **Ronny**.

**Ronny**    Oh dear. (*Pause.*) Would you like a bridge party?

**Adela**    You mean you would like us to play cards with
them. (*Sits at the card table with* **Mrs Moore**.)

**Ronny**   No, our civil administrator, Mr Turton, has
concocted this idea of bridge parties – a party to bridge the
gulf between East and West. The expression is his own
invention.

**Adela**   I only want to meet those Indians you come across
socially – as your friends.

**Ronny**   Well, we don't come across them socially except
at an event like a . . .

**Mrs Moore**   Bridge party.

**Ronny**   Yes, Mother.

**Adela**   I would so like that, Ronny. (*Pats his hand.*) You are
really very thoughtful.

**Ronny**   Thank you, Adela. (*An uncomfortable pause.*) I think
perhaps I should retire.

*He kisses his mother on her forehead, then notices something on the side
of her chair, and picks up a brochure which he raises above his head, as
if to strike.*

**Mrs Moore**   Good heavens. What is it?

**Ronny**   Just a wasp.

**Mrs Moore**   No, no, leave it. Please.

**Ronny** *lowers the brochure.* **Mrs Moore** *squeezes his hand.*

**Mrs Moore**   Goodnight.

**Ronny** *bows to* **Adela**.

**Ronny**   Adela.

**Adela**   Ronny.

**Ronny** *leaves.*

**Mrs Moore** *looks at the wasp on the arm of her chair.*

**Mrs Moore**   Pretty dear.

**Aziz** *runs on with a bicycle which he places on the ground. He rushes into* **Hamidullah**'s *house.*

**Aziz**    Hamidullah! Hamidullah! Am I late?

*He finds* **Hamidullah** *and* **Mahmoud Ali**, *both dressed in orthodox Moslem clothing, on the veranda, sitting in front of a hookah.*

**Hamidullah**    Do not apologise. You are always late.

**Aziz**    But it has been a difficult day. One ruptured appendix, one hernia . . .

**Hamidullah**    Please, spare us the details. We do not entertain you with the minutiae of our day in the law courts.

**Aziz**    Has Mahmoud Ali eaten all the food? If so I go elsewhere. Mr Mahmoud Ali, how are you?

**Mahmoud Ali**    Thank you, Dr Aziz, I am dying.

**Aziz**    Dying before dinner? Oh, poor Mahmoud Ali.

**Hamidullah**    Aziz, don't chatter. We are having an important talk. We are discussing whether or not it is possible to be friends with an Englishman. I have received an invitation, as has Mahmoud Ali, as I'm sure you have, to join Mr Turton in the garden of the club between the hours of five and seven on Tuesday.

**Aziz**    Ah, yes. Those are busy hours for me at the hospital. I doubt that I will attend.

**Hamidullah**    Did you know that when Turton first came out to assume his post, I drove with him in his carriage – oh yes, Turton! We were quite intimate. He showed me his stamp collection.

**Mahmoud Ali**    Now he would expect you to steal it.

**Hamidullah**    They all become exactly the same. I give any Englishman two years. And I give any Englishwoman two months. Do you not agree with me?

**Mahmoud Ali**    I do not. I find them not the same at all. That new magistrate mumbles, for instance. Whereas Turton talks distinctly. If you study them carefully, you can spot these differences. Mr Turton pretends towards integrity, while his wife quite openly takes bribes.

**Hamidullah**    Bribes?

**Mahmoud Ali**    Did you not know that when the canal scheme was proposed, some raja or other gave her a sewing machine in solid gold so that the water should run through his state.

**Hamidullah**    And does it?

**Mahmoud Ali**    Of course not. That is where Mrs Turton is so skilful. When we blacks take bribes, we perform what we are bribed to perform. The English take bribes but then do nothing. I admire them.

**Aziz**    Mrs Turton, to be quite candid, had a beautifully formed gall bladder.

*They laugh.* **Aziz** *passes the hookah to* **Hamidullah**.

**Hamidullah**    You are generous about our English friends, Aziz; indeed you have a tenderness for most everyone . . .

**Aziz**    Not Major Callender and his wife.

**Hamidullah**    The Callenders excepted.

**Aziz**    Because I know at the bottom of my heart that the English cannot help being so cold and odd. It is not their fault. They were created that way. I object only to the time we spend talking about them. We could instead be reciting poems. Listen . . .

*He recites a Persian poem. He is in love with the poem; the words sing on his lips.*

**Hamidullah** *and* **Mahmoud Ali** *listen.* **Aziz** *finishes. They are all in a stupor. There is a sense of perfect happiness.*

**Aziz**   And this . . .

*He recites another poem. The hookah is passed.*

**Hamidullah** (*in a trance*)   Words, words . . .

**Aziz**   I breathe them like the night air. . .

**Mahmoud Ali**   The poets, Hafiz, Hali, Iqbal . . .

**Hamidullah**   A hundred languages. A hundred Indias . . .

**Aziz**   No, tonight there is only one India – my own . . .
(*He smiles in satisfaction.*)

*The bridge party.*

*The club lawn.* **Mr** *and* **Mrs Turton**, **Major Callender**,
*and* **Mr Burton** *stand drinking tea on one side of the lawn,
surrounded by other* **Members** *of the club.* **Ronny** *is with them,
and an extremely awkward* **Adela** *and* **Mrs Moore**. *The*
**Indians** *stand on the other side of the lawn, but we cannot see them.
The* **English** *stare out at the audience as if they were looking at the*
**Indians**. *There is no effort to communicate.*

**Ronny** (*to* **Turton**)   It was very kind of you to arrange this
party, sir.

**Turton**   It's a pleasure, my boy.

**Ronny** (*to* **Adela**)   Of course, the truth is that no one
who's here matters; those who matter don't come. Isn't that
so, Mrs Turton?

**Mrs Turton**   Absolutely true. If only one could avoid an
afternoon like this.

**Turton** (*looking across to the* **Indians**)   Well, well . . . who
have we so far? Hmm. Much as one expected. We know
why that one's here – over that contract, and next to him is
the astrologer who wants to bypass the municipal building
regulations, and over there that Parsee with the family
dispute . . . rather the turnout one expected. No surprises.
Hello! What's this? One of them has driven his carriage into

our hollyhocks. Pulled his horse's left rein when he meant the right. All as usual.

**Mrs Turton**   They ought never to have been allowed to drive in; it's so bad for them.

**Burton**   Why they come at all I don't know. They hate it as much as we do.

**Turton** (*to* **Adela**)   Aside from a few broken blossoms, Miss Quested, it's hardly picturesque, I'm afraid.

**Adela**   Everyone seems so pleasant.

**Mrs Turton**   Natives don't respect one any the more after meeting one, you know. I was a nurse before my marriage and came across them a great deal, so I know. One has to stay firmly aloof.

**Adela**   Even from one's patients?

**Burton**   The kindest thing one can do to a native is to let him die.

**Mrs Moore**   And then if he goes to heaven?

**Major Callender**   He can go where he likes as long as he doesn't come near me.

**Mrs Turton**   I take your point about heaven. It's made me think.

**Mrs Moore**   *Has* it?

**Mrs Turton**   Yes. And that is why I am against missionaries.

**Adela**   Well, I think instead of standing around staring at them, we should introduce ourselves. I notice that the schoolmaster has already done so. Are you coming, Mrs Moore?

**Mrs Moore**   With pleasure.

**Adela** *and* **Mrs Moore** *march off, followed by an embarrassed* **Ronny**.

**Mrs Turton**   Miss Quested, what a name! I hope she hasn't been brought out to marry nice little Heaslop. It seems she comes from Hampstead. Mixes with a literary set.

**Major Callender**   Oh dear, oh dear. I say, she's talking to quite a few of them, as is that schoolmaster.

**Turton**   Fielding's quite a decent chap, actually. (*Indicates with a shake of his head that he sees* **Fielding** *mixing with the* **Indians**.)

**Mrs Turton**   Fielding! He's not pukka, never will be. *He* should marry Miss Quested.

**Major Callender**   They seem to be talking to most anyone.

**Turton**   Right. Time to do our duty. To work, Mary, to work!

**Mrs Turton**   What do you want me to do? Oh, those purdah women! I never thought any would come. Oh dear!

**Turton**   Come along, Mary, get it over.

*The* **English** *turn around and are transformed into the* **Indians**, *talking in a crowd to* **Adela** *and* **Mrs Moore**.

**Mrs Moore** (*to an Indian woman,* **Mrs Bhattacharya**) I'm so sorry we don't speak your language . . .

**Mrs Bhattacharya**   We speak a little of yours.

**Adela**   How lovely.

**Indian Man**   Eastbourne. Piccadilly. High Park Corner.

**Mrs Bhattacharya**   Some of us a little more, some a little less. (*They laugh.*)

**Adela** *and* **Mrs Moore** *move with the* **Indians** *in a circle;* **Fielding** *is in a concurrent one. Chatter. The sun is blazing.*

**Adela** *is feeling the heat. Suddenly everything and everyone around her seems to fade. Reality disappears. It is dark and frightening.*

*And then, just as suddenly, she snaps back, and it is light. She is facing hills that lie in the distance. She is alone, except for* **Fielding**, *who is standing behind her.*

**Fielding**   Those are the Marabar Hills.

**Adela**   They look so close.

**Fielding**   Far away, actually.

**Adela**   Really?

**Fielding**   I promise.

**Adela**   They seem so peaceful.

**Fielding** (*holds out his hand*)   Cyril Fielding.

**Adela** (*shaking his hand*)   Adela Quested. You're the schoolmaster. I've heard about you.

**Fielding** (*smiles*)   Yes. (*Pause.*) I'm afraid sunsets are very swift in the tropics.

**Adela**   The bridge party hasn't been very successful, has it?

**Fielding**   Well, you and Mrs Moore were not a failure. You actually broke quite a few conventions – you were friendly and polite – and our guests were very impressed. As was I.

**Adela**   You circulated freely as well.

**Fielding**   Yes, and it displeases some, but I can't be sacked from my job because my job is education. (*Pause.*) I'm rather a hermit, you know.

**Adela**   Much the best thing to be in this place.

**Fielding**   I don't get up too much to the club.

**Adela**   And we never get down from it. (*Pause.*) I can see what a life is like out here. Looking into the club every evening, then driving home to dress. Seeing the Turtons and the Callenders and the McBrydes. Inviting them and being invited by them. A life. (*Pause.*) While India slides by unnoticed.

**Fielding**    Then I would like very much to invite you and Mrs Moore to tea. And perhaps a few Indians as well.

**Adela**    Oh, I would like that and so too would Mrs Moore, I know.

**Fielding**    Do you care about Indian music? There is an old professor down at the college who sings.

**Adela**    Oh, just what we would want to hear. And do you know Dr Aziz?

**Fielding**    I know all about him. I don't know him. Would you like him asked too?

**Adela**    Mrs Moore says he is so nice.

**Fielding**    Very well, Miss Quested. Shall we plan on Thursday?

*She turns to view the hills.*

**Godbole**, *holding an invitation.*

**Godbole**    I chose a purple turban. It was important to consider the colour. A coat, of course, a waistcoat, dhoti, and socks with a special design – clocks. Purple clocks. They created the appearance of harmony. Or of time standing still. (*He looks at the invitation again.*)

**Aziz** *is also reading an invitation. He takes off his doctor's uniform and puts on regular dress. He combs his hair. He is beside himself with excitement.*

**Aziz** *arrives at* **Fielding**'s *house.*

**Fielding** *is inside, dressing after a bath. His* **Servant** *announces:*

**Servant**    Dr Aziz.

**Aziz** *enters the living room. He cannot see* **Fielding** *who is in his dressing room.*

**Fielding**   Please make yourself at home.

**Aziz**   May I really, Mr Fielding? It's very good of you.
I like unconventional behaviour so extremely. The fact is
I have long wanted to meet you – I have heard so much
about your warm heart. But where is one to meet in a
wretched hole like Chandrapore? (*Walks close to the partition.*)
When I was greener here, I'll tell you what; I used to wish
you to fall ill so we could meet that way. Then we would
have had jolly talks for you are a celebrated student of
Persian poetry.

**Fielding**   You know me by sight, then?

**Aziz**   Of course, of course. You know me?

**Fielding**   I know you very well by name.

**Aziz**   I say, Mr Fielding.

**Fielding**   Yes?

**Aziz**   Guess what I look like before you come out. That
will be a kind of game.

**Fielding** *is able to glimpse an image – or a shadow of* **Aziz** *–
through the partition.*

**Fielding**   You have a slim build.

**Aziz**   Jolly good. What next? Do I have a venerable white
beard?

**Fielding**   Blast!

**Aziz**   Anything wrong?

**Fielding**   I've stamped on my last collar stud.

**Aziz**   Take mine, take mine.

**Fielding**   Have you a spare one?

**Aziz**   Yes, yes, one minute.

**Fielding**   Not if you're wearing it yourself.

**Aziz**    No, no, one in my pocket.

**Aziz** *moves to the side and wrenches off his collar. He pulls a gold stud out of the back of his collar.*

**Aziz**    Here it is.

**Fielding**    Come in with it if you don't mind the unconventionality.

**Aziz** (*replaces his collar*)    One minute again.

**Aziz** *walks into the other room and hands* **Fielding** *the stud.*

**Fielding**    Many thanks. ·

*They shake hands, smiling.* **Aziz** *looks around the room.*

**Aziz**    But I always thought that Englishmen kept their rooms so tidy. It seems this is not so. Everything arranged coldly on shelves is what I imagined. Is the stud going to go in?

**Fielding**    I have my doubts.

**Aziz**    Let me . . . I see . . . the hole is small..

**Fielding**    Why in hell does one wear collars at all?

**Aziz**    We wear them to pass the police.

**Fielding**    What's that?

**Aziz**    If I'm biking in English dress they take no notice. When I wear a fez they pull me over. Hooray! She's gone in! Sometimes I shut my eyes and dream I have splendid clothes and am riding into battle behind Alamgir.

**Fielding**    Ah, Alamgir.

**Aziz**    Must not India have been beautiful then with the Mogul Empire at its height and Alamgir reigning at Delhi upon the Peacock Throne?

**Aziz** *recites a Persian poem.* **Adela** *and* **Mrs Moore** *enter as he is reciting.* **Adela** *looks at* **Aziz**, *eyes wide, drinking in the poem.* **Fielding** *leads them to their seats.* **Adela** *now closes her eyes and*

*lets the words drift over her. Persian music is heard.* **Godbole**
*interrupts her reverie, walking through the centre, carrying a tea tray.*

*The music has disappeared. They are seated now.* **Fielding**, **Aziz**,
**Adela** *and* **Mrs Moore** *drinking tea.* **Godbole** *takes his tea
from a low table placed slightly behind him, to which he stretches back.
He eats and smiles, eats and smiles, and says nothing. They are
smoking.* **Aziz** *has been talking a blue streak.*

**Aziz**    You remember the water by our mosque, Mrs
Moore? It comes down from the mosque to this very garden
and fills the tank outside – a skilful arrangement of the
emperors. They stopped here going down into Bengal. They
loved water. Wherever they went they created fountains,
gardens, hammans.

**Mrs Moore**    But how does the water gravitate uphill?

**Aziz** (*stumped, for his facts are incorrect*)    A mystery.

**Adela**    I do so hate mysteries.

**Mrs Moore**    I like mysteries. But I rather dislike muddles.

**Fielding**    A mystery is a muddle.

**Mrs Moore**    Oh, do you think so, Mr Fielding?

**Fielding**    A mystery is only a high-sounding term for a
muddle. Aziz and I know well that India is a muddle.

**Adela**    Oh, but a beautiful one, I imagine.

**Aziz**    Why not settle altogether in India?

**Adela**    No, I'm afraid I can't do that.

**Aziz**    But you are not leaving us so soon?

**Adela** (*flustered*)    Oh no . . . I didn't mean that exactly.

**Aziz**    Visitors like you are too rare.

**Adela**    We've seen so little.

**Fielding**    Perhaps the ladies would like to view the college
grounds.

**Mrs Moore**    I'd be delighted to. May we?

*Everyone rises except for* **Godbole** *who is finishing a banana.*

**Mrs Moore**    Don't you come too, Adela; you dislike institutions.

**Adela**    Yes, that is so.

**Adela** *sits again.* **Mrs Moore** *and* **Fielding** *walk out through the garden.* **Aziz** *is disconcerted at being alone with* **Adela** *and* **Godbole**.

**Aziz**    May I offer you . . . (*Holds out cigarettes.*)

**Adela** (*takes one*)    Oh yes, thank you . . .

*An awkward silence, as he lights her cigarette. They smoke.*

**Aziz**    Miss Quested, Professor Godbole brought delicious sweets. You must try them. They will give you a real Indian treat. Ah, in my poor position I can give you nothing. No – no – that is not true. I hereby invite you all to see me in the Marabar Caves. Yes!

**Adela**    I shall be delighted.

**Aziz** (*surprised*)    Oh. (*Pause.*) Unless you have visited them before?

**Adela**    No, I've not even heard of them.

**Aziz**    Not heard of them? The Marabar Caves in the Marabar Hills?

**Adela**    We hear nothing interesting up at the club. Tell me everything you will, or I shall never understand India. What are these caves?

**Aziz**    Actually, I've not been there myself. I've always been meaning to go but work has prevented me.

**Adela**    Are they large caves?

**Aziz** *hesitates – he hasn't a clue.* **Godbole** *looks up.*

**Godbole**    No, not large.

**Adela**    Do describe them, Professor Godbole,

**Godbole**    It will be a great honour. (*Draws up his chair.*)
There is an entrance in the rock, where you enter. (*Pause.*)

**Adela**    Yes?

**Godbole**    And through the entrance is the cave.

**Adela**    Something like the caves at Elefanta?

**Godbole**    Oh no, not at all. At Elefanta there are
sculptures of Siva and Parvati. There are no sculptures at all
at Marabar.

**Aziz**    They are immensely holy, no doubt.

**Godbole**    Oh no, oh no.

**Aziz**    Still they are ornamented in some way.

**Godbole**    Oh no.

**Aziz**    Well, why are they so famous? We all talk of the
famous Marabar Caves. Perhaps that is our empty brag.

**Godbole**    No, I should not quite say that.

**Aziz**    Describe them to the lady, then.

**Godbole**    It will be a great pleasure. (*Takes a mango.*)
Mango season is almost over.

*A long pause.*

**Aziz**    When I was a boy I used to run out to a big mango
grove and gorge myself. My friends as well. Sometimes we
would lie in the field, wet from the rain, our bodies covered
with mango juice. We all ended up with painful stomachs.
We have a proverb in Urdu – 'What does unhappiness
matter when we are all unhappy together?'

*He looks at* **Adela**. **Adela**, *embarrassed, turns away.*

**Adela**    I've never tasted a mango.

**Godbole**    (*holds out a mango*)    Please . . .

**Adela** *takes one.* **Ronny** *enters, followed by* **Fielding**'s
**Servant**. *He addresses* **Adela** *and does not acknowledge* **Aziz** *or*
**Godbole**.

**Ronny**    What's happened to Fielding? Where's my
mother?

**Adela** (*coolly*)    Good evening.

**Ronny**    I want you and Mother at once. There's to be
polo.

**Godbole** (*rises*)    Your mother will return shortly, sir. There
is but little to see at our poor college.

**Ronny** (*ignoring him*)    I left work at an early hour because I
thought the polo would give you pleasure.

**Aziz**    Come along and join us, Mr Heaslop. Sit down till
your mother shows up.

**Ronny** (*to* **Servant**)    Please fetch your master at once.

**Aziz**    Allow me. (*He repeats the phrase to the* **Servant** *in his
native tongue.* **Ronny** *frowns.*) Ah – here they are at any rate.

**Fielding** *and* **Mrs Moore** *come in from the garden.*

**Ronny**    Don't trouble to come in, Mother. We're just
leaving.

**Aziz** *goes to* **Mrs Moore**. **Ronny** *takes* **Fielding** *aside.*

**Ronny**    I say, old man, do excuse me, but I think you
probably oughtn't to have left Miss Quested alone.

**Fielding**    I'm sorry, what's up?

**Ronny**    Well . . . I'm the sun-dried bureaucrat, no doubt,
still I don't like to see an English girl left smoking with two
Indians.

**Fielding**    She stops, as she smokes, by her own wish, old
man.

**Ronny**    Yes, that's all right in England.

**Fielding**   I really can't see the harm.

**Ronny**   Can't you see that fellow's a bounder?

**Fielding**   He isn't a bounder. His nerves seem a bit on edge, that's all.

**Ronny**   What should have upset his precious nerves?

**Fielding**   I don't know. He was all right when I left.

**Ronny**   Well, it's nothing I said. I never even spoke to him.

**Fielding**   Oh well, come along now, and take your ladies away; the catastrophe's over.

**Ronny**   Fielding, don't think I'm taking it badly, or anything of that sort . . . I suppose you won't come on to the polo with us? We should all be delighted.

**Fielding**   I'm afraid I can't, thanks all the same. I'm awfully sorry you feel I've been remiss. I didn't mean to be.

**Mrs Moore**   Goodbye, Mr Fielding, and thank you so much . . . what lovely college buildings.

**Fielding**   Goodbye, Mrs Moore.

**Adela**   Goodbye, Mr Fielding. Such an interesting afternoon.

**Fielding**   Goodbye, Miss Quested.

**Mrs Moore**   Goodbye, Dr Aziz.

**Aziz**   Goodbye, Mrs Moore.

**Adela**   Goodbye, Dr Aziz.

**Aziz**   Goodbye, Miss Quested. You'll jolly, jolly well not forget those caves, won't you? I'll fix the whole show up in a jiffy.

**Adela**   Thank you.

**Aziz**    What a shame you leave India so soon! Oh, do reconsider your decision. Do stay.

**Ronny** (*puzzled*)    Adela?

**Adela**, *embarrassed, doesn't look at* **Ronny***: she vigorously shakes* **Godbole***'s hand.*

**Adela**    Goodbye, Professor Godbole. It's a shame we never heard you sing.

**Godbole**    I may sing now. (*Clears his throat.*)

**Adela**    Oh.

**Ronny**    Blast.

**Godbole** *sings. There is only an occasional illusion of a Western melody. The sound of his voice is hypnotic. It casts a spell over all except* **Ronny** *who, finally, bored and testy, walks into the garden.*

**Adela** *is transported by the music into another world. She is carried away by the sensuality of the music. She closes her eyes. She sees an image of two boys, almost naked, wet with rain and mango juice, wrestling in a field.*

*She gasps. She is back in* **Fielding***'s room listening to* **Godbole** *sing.*

**Godbole** *stops halfway through a bar and sits down.*

**Fielding**    Thanks so much; what was that?

**Godbole**    I will explain in detail. It was a religious song. I placed myself in the position of a milk maiden. I say to Shri Krishna, 'Come! Come to me only.' The God refuses to come. I grow humble and say, 'Do not come to me only. Multiply yourself into a hundred Krishnas, and let one go to each of my hundred companions, but let one, O Lord of the Universe, one, come to me.' He refuses to come.

**Mrs Moore**    But he comes in some other way, I hope.

**Godbole**   Oh no. He refuses to come. I say to him,
'Come, come, come, come, come, come . . .' He neglects to
come.

**Mrs Moore**   Yes. I see. There is not enough God to go
around.

**Godbole** *smiles*.

*Riding in a tum-tum.* **Mrs Moore** *sits in the front, next to a*
**Driver**. **Ronny** *and* **Adela** *are in the back seat.*

**Ronny**   What was that about caves?

**Adela**   Mrs Moore, your doctor, whom I find delightful,
has decided to invite us to a picnic out there – you, myself,
Mr Fielding, Professor Godbole – exactly the same party.

**Ronny**   Out where?

**Adela**   The Marabar Caves.

**Ronny**   Well I'm blessed. Did he descend to any details?

**Adela**   He did not. If you had spoken to him, we could
have arranged them. (**Ronny** *shakes his head, laughing*.) Have I
said anything funny?

**Ronny**   I was only thinking how your worthy doctor's
collar climbed up his neck.

**Adela**   I thought we were discussing the caves.

**Ronny**   So I am. Aziz was exquisitely dressed, but he had
forgotten his back collar stud, and there you have the
Indians all over; inattention to detail.

**Mrs Moore**   I like Aziz. Aziz is my real friend.

**Ronny**   My point is they are unreliable. And naive. For
instance, to 'meet' in the caves as if they were the clock at
Charing Cross, when they're miles from a station and each
other.

**Adela**   Have you been to them?

**Ronny**    No, but I know all about them, naturally.

**Adela**    Oh, naturally!

**Ronny**    Are you pledged to this expedition, Mother?

**Mrs Moore**    Mother is pledged to nothing. Certainly not to this polo. I've never heard of these caves. I don't know what or where they are. But I really can't have so much quarrelling and tiresomeness. I want to be left off at the bungalow. Stop here.

*The tum-tum stops. She stares at* **Ronny** *and* **Adela**.

I feel increasingly that though people are important, the relations between them are not.

**Ronny**, *ashamed, helps her down. A* **Servant** *comes out to walk* **Mrs Moore** *back to the house.* **Ronny** *returns to the back seat.*

**Ronny** (*to* **Driver**)    We'll go to the club now. (*The* **Driver** *doesn't respond.*) Damn. Not a word of English. Club. Club! (*The* **Driver** *starts again.*)

**Adela**    We must have a thorough talk, Ronny, I'm afraid.

**Ronny**    My temper's rotten, I must apologise. I didn't mean to order you and Mother about, but I know this Aziz will make some muddle over the caves.

**Adela**    It's something very different, nothing to do with the caves, that I wanted to talk over with you. I've finally decided that we are not going to be married, dear boy.

**Ronny** (*pause – quietly*)    You never said we should marry, my dear girl; you never bound either yourself or me – don't let this upset you.

**Adela**    But let us discuss things; it's all so frightfully important, we mustn't make false steps. I want next to hear your point of view about me – it might help us both.

**Ronny**    I don't much believe in this discussing.

**Adela**　I only want everything to be absolutely clear between us and to answer any questions you care to put to me on my conduct.

**Ronny**　But I haven't any questions. You've acted within your rights. You were quite right to come out and have a look at me doing my work, and anyhow, it's no use talking further – we should only get up steam.

**Adela**　We've been awfully British over it, but I suppose that's all right.

**Ronny**　As we are British, I suppose it is.

**Adela**　Anyhow, we've not quarrelled, Ronny.

**Ronny**　Oh, that would have been too absurd. Why should we quarrel?

**Adela**　I think we shall keep friends.

**Ronny**　I know we shall.

**Adela**　Quite so.

**Adela** *fishes out a cigarette.*

**Adela**　Let's not go to the club.

**Ronny**　Shall I take you home?

**Adela**　No. A drive. Fresh air.

**Ronny** (*to* **Driver**)　No club. No club. (*Pantomimes.*) Drive. Country. Ganauati Road. No, no, sorry, it's under repair. Marabar Road.

**Driver**　Ah. Marabar Road.

**Adela**　Thank you. (*Pause.*) Oh. Listen . . .

**Ronny**　What?

**Adela**　To that bird. Did you hear it?

**Ronny**　Yes.

**Adela**　What do you think it was called?

**Ronny**    I'm afraid I'm not good at birds; in fact, I'm useless at any information outside my own job.

**Adela**    So am I. I'm useless at everything.

**Ronny** and **Adela** *sit stiffly next to each other, unable to converse any more.* **Godbole**'s *song is heard in the faint distance.*

*They hear the rustle of trees which seem to be calling to them: Come, come, come, come, come, come . . .*

**Aziz** *appears in the front seat again, and turns and looks at* **Adela**. *He disappears. Darkness falls. The night is suddenly mysterious. A jolt.* **Adela**'s *hand accidentally touches* **Ronny**'s. *An intangible thrill seizes them. Neither withdraws their hand. They are surrounded by stars. But there are ominous shadows in the darkness.*

*Suddenly – bump, jump, a swerve, the wheels lift in the air, brakes on, stand still.* **Adela** *grips* **Ronny**'s *hand, tightly.*

**Ronny**    What's the damage?

*The* **Driver** *shouts in Urdu.*

**Ronny**    Frightened, Adela?

**Adela**    Not a bit.

**Ronny**    Well, it's all over now. We skidded, I imagine.

**Adela**    We didn't skid. We ran into an animal.

**Ronny**    An animal?

**Adela**    A large animal rushed up out of the dark on the right and hit us.

**Ronny**    I didn't see an animal . . .

*Pause;* **Adela** *looks at him.*

. . . but, of course, if you say there was one, then, indeed there was one. (*Gets out and examines the right side of the car.*) Look, the paint's gone. It might have been a falling rock.

**Adela**    I saw a hairy back quite plainly.

**Ronny**   I say, Adela, what was it?

**Adela**   I don't know the animals any better than the birds here – too big for a goat.

**Ronny**   Let's look for its tracks.

**Adela** *and* **Ronny** *leave the car. The* **Driver** *hands them a torch.* **Ronny** *and* **Adela** *examine the ground near the car. They are a bit like children now.*

**Ronny**   Do you think it was a buffalo?

**Adela** (*thrilled*)   A buffalo? Perhaps.

**Ronny** (*searching for tracks*)   Buffalo . . .

**Adela**   Unless it was a hyena.

**Ronny**   Hyena?

**Adela** (*smiles*)   Yes, a hyena.

**Ronny**   There aren't any tracks that are legible . . .

*Another car approaches from the opposite side.* **Ronny** *hails it.* **Miss Derek***, a sporty young Englishwoman, sits inside.*

**Ronny**   We've had a breakdown.

**Miss Derek**   But how putrid!

**Ronny**   We ran into a hyena.

**Miss Derek**   How absolutely rotten.

**Ronny**   Miss Derek. This is Miss Quested . . .

**Adela**   Lovely to meet you.

**Miss Derek**   What an adventure, eh?

**Ronny**   Can you give us a lift?

**Miss Derek**   Yes indeed . . .

**Ronny** *and* **Adela** *enter her car. They notice a dog asleep on the front seat. They sit in the back.* **Miss Derek** *starts her car again.*

Actually, the West doesn't bother much about
lisbelief in these days.

**ullah**   Excuse the question, but how is a country
eal belief justified in holding India?

**g**   I'm out here personally because I needed a job.
 tell you why England is here or whether she ought
 e.

**llah**   Then excuse me again – is it fair that
 en should occupy jobs when well-qualified Indians
 able? Of course, I mean nothing personally.
 ly we are delighted you should be here.

**g**   I'm delighted to be here too – that's my answer,
 only excuse. I can't tell you anything about

**ullah**   And these Englishmen who are not
 l to be here – have they an excuse?

**g**   None. Chuck 'em out. (*They look at him amazed.*)
 poken out of turn?

**ullah**   You bewilder and amaze us, Mr Fielding.
 so frank. For us, what we say and what we feel are
 he same.

**g**   Then you resemble your rulers, don't you think?

 Rafi, Rafi!

 Dr Aziz?

 You sit on my leg.

**ullah**   Come along, we tire the invalid.

**oud Ali**   Yes, we must conclude our visit.

 Thank you, gentlemen. But Mr Fielding, may you
 moment?

**g**   Certainly.

*She waves to the hapless* **Driver**, *left stranded on the road as she speeds off.*

**Miss Derek**   Cheerio! (*To* **Ronny** *and* **Adela**.) I've stolen the Maharaja's car. I'm companion to a maharanee, Miss Quested, in one of the Native States. She's an absolute dear, but he'll be very put out. (*Motions towards the dog.*) That's his fox terrier by the way. It's just that I needed a car for my holiday. I suppose he'll sack me, but if so, I'll get another job. The whole of India just seethes with maharanees and ronis and begums who clamour for such as me.

**Ronny**   Really, I had no idea.

**Miss Derek**   How could you have any idea, Mr Heaslop? What should he know about maharanees or the Hindu States.

**Adela**   I understand those big people are not particularly interesting.

**Adela** *takes* **Ronny***'s hand and squeezes it to signal her amusement at* **Miss Derek**. **Ronny** *smiles.*

**Miss Derek**   Ah, there you are wrong. They're priceless. They're all quite eccentric, you know.

**Adela** *and* **Ronny** *laugh.* **Adela** *turns to* **Ronny** *nervously and says quietly:*

**Adela**   Ronny, what I said earlier. . . you know. . .

**Ronny**   Yes?

**Adela**   I would like to take it back.

**Ronny**   Oh, I'm so pleased. (*He smiles in relief, and squeezes her hand especially tight. Her other hand moves as if to touch him, but then modestly drops into her lap.*)

**Mrs Moore**, *in her room, writing a letter.*

**Mrs Moore**   Dear Stella, dear Ralph, It seems my duties have finished now. Ronny is suited and after the wedding I shall return home. I don't want to see India now, not really.

*She waves to the hapless* **Driver**, *left stranded on the road as she speeds off.*

**Miss Derek**   Cheerio! (*To* **Ronny** *and* **Adela**.) I've stolen the Maharaja's car. I'm companion to a maharanee, Miss Quested, in one of the Native States. She's an absolute dear, but he'll be very put out. (*Motions towards the dog.*) That's his fox terrier by the way. It's just that I needed a car for my holiday. I suppose he'll sack me, but if so, I'll get another job. The whole of India just seethes with maharanees and ronis and begums who clamour for such as me.

**Ronny**   Really, I had no idea.

**Miss Derek**   How could you have any idea, Mr Heaslop? What should he know about maharanees or the Hindu States.

**Adela**   I understand those big people are not particularly interesting.

**Adela** *takes* **Ronny**'s *hand and squeezes it to signal her amusement at* **Miss Derek**. **Ronny** *smiles.*

**Miss Derek**   Ah, there you are wrong. They're priceless. They're all quite eccentric, you know.

**Adela** *and* **Ronny** *laugh.* **Adela** *turns to* **Ronny** *nervously and says quietly:*

**Adela**   Ronny, what I said earlier. . . you know. . .

**Ronny**   Yes?

**Adela**   I would like to take it back.

**Ronny**   Oh, I'm so pleased. (*He smiles in relief, and squeezes her hand especially tight. Her other hand moves as if to touch him, but then modestly drops into her lap.*)

**Mrs Moore**, *in her room, writing a letter.*

**Mrs Moore**   Dear Stella, dear Ralph, It seems my duties have finished now. Ronny is suited and after the wedding I shall return home. I don't want to see India now, not really.

I did so wish to say something enthusiastic – or encouraging
– to Ronny and Adela about marriage, but I didn't know
what. I rather feel that too much fuss is made over marriage;
centuries of carnal embracement, yet man is no nearer to
understanding man. Of course I said nothing of the sort.
What is there to say – really – about anything? (*She pauses
and then rips the letter in two.*)

**Godbole**'s *song is heard.*

**Aziz** *wakes up in bed sweating.* **Godbole**'s *song fades away.*

**Aziz** *in bed.* **Hamidullah** *enters with* **Mahmoud Ali** *and*
**Rafi**, *his nephew.*

**Hamidullah**   Aziz, my dear fellow, we are greatly
concerned.

**Mahmoud Ali**   When a doctor falls ill, it is a serious
matter.

*The three men sit on* **Aziz**'s *bed.*

**Rafi**   Dr Aziz took tea with our Mr Fielding last Thursday
afternoon. Professor Godbole, who also attended, has
sickened too, which seems a curious thing, does it not?

**Aziz**   How do you do, young Rafi. How very kind of you
to enquire after my health. How do you do, Hamidullah?
But you bring me bad news. What is wrong with Godbole?

**Hamidullah**   Why don't you answer, Rafi. You're the
great authority.

**Mahmoud Ali**   Yes, Rafi is the Sherlock Holmes of
Chandrapore.

**Rafi**   Diarrhoea.

**Aziz**   If this is so, this is a very serious thing; diarrhoea
before the end of March. Why have I not been informed?

**Rafi**   Dr Panna Lal attends him, sir.

**Aziz**   Oh yes, they are both Hindus; there we have it; they hang together like flies and keep everything dark. Rafi, tell me all the details. Is there vomiting also?

**Rafi**   Oh yes, indeed, sir, and the stomach pains.

**Aziz**   Alla! That settles it. In twenty-four hours he will be dead.

**Mahmoud Ali**   All illness proceeds from Hindus.

**Fielding** *bursts into the room. The other visitors stand.*

**Fielding**   I say, is he ill, or isn't he ill?

**Aziz** (*to the others*)   Sit down.

**Mahmoud Ali**   It is good of Mr Fielding to condescend to visit our friend. We are touched by this great kindness.

**Aziz**   Don't talk to him like that, he doesn't want it.

**Fielding**   Well, are you ill, Aziz, or aren't you?

**Aziz**   We should be more concerned about Professor Godbole.

**Fielding**   Oh yes. Poor chap evidently has haemorrhoids.

**Aziz** (*laughing, to* **Rafi**)   Haemorrhoids – so much, my dear Sherlock, for your cholera.

**Rafi**   But I never said the word cholera.

**Hamidullah**   Dr Aziz is ill and he is not ill. And I suppose that most of us are in that same case. The whole world looks to be dying, still it doesn't die, so we must assume the existence of a beneficent Providence.

**Fielding**   I'm afraid I don't believe in Providence.

**Mahmoud Ali**   But how then can you believe in God?

**Fielding**   I don't.

**Hamidullah**   Is it correct that most are atheists in England now?

**Fielding**    Actually, the West doesn't bother much about belief or disbelief in these days.

**Hamidullah**    Excuse the question, but how is a country without real belief justified in holding India?

**Fielding**    I'm out here personally because I needed a job. I cannot tell you why England is here or whether she ought to be here.

**Hamidullah**    Then excuse me again – is it fair that Englishmen should occupy jobs when well-qualified Indians are available? Of course, I mean nothing personally. Personally we are delighted you should be here.

**Fielding**    I'm delighted to be here too – that's my answer, that's my only excuse. I can't tell you anything about fairness.

**Hamidullah**    And these Englishmen who are not delighted to be here – have they an excuse?

**Fielding**    None. Chuck 'em out. (*They look at him amazed.*) Have I spoken out of turn?

**Hamidullah**    You bewilder and amaze us, Mr Fielding. You are so frank. For us, what we say and what we feel are seldom the same.

**Fielding**    Then you resemble your rulers, don't you think?

**Aziz**    Rafi, Rafi!

**Rafi**    Dr Aziz?

**Aziz**    You sit on my leg.

**Hamidullah**    Come along, we tire the invalid.

**Mahmoud Ali**    Yes, we must conclude our visit.

**Aziz**    Thank you, gentlemen. But Mr Fielding, may you linger a moment?

**Fielding**    Certainly.

**Hamidullah**, **Mahmoud Ali** *and* **Rafi** *leave.*

**Aziz**    Before you go, will you please unlock that drawer.

**Fielding**    Where is the key?

**Aziz**    Here. Round my neck. (*Points to a key that rests on a string around his neck.*) Please.

**Fielding** *is very hesitant; but then he removes the string from* **Aziz***'s neck.*

**Aziz**    The drawer. Please.

**Fielding**    Are you certain?

**Aziz**    Yes. Of course. What is the problem?

**Fielding** *goes to the drawer and opens it with the key.*

**Aziz**    Do you see a piece of brown paper at the top?

**Fielding**    Yes.

**Aziz**    Open it.

**Fielding** (*removes a photograph*)    Who is this?

**Aziz**    She was my wife. You are the first Englishman she has ever come before. Now put her photograph away.

**Fielding** (*astonished, murmurs*)    Really, I don't know why you pay me this great compliment, Aziz, but I do appreciate it.

**Aziz**    You would have seen her, so why should you not see her photograph?

**Fielding**    You would have allowed me to meet her?

**Aziz**    Why not? All men are my brothers, and as soon as one behaves as such he may see my wife.

**Fielding**    And when the whole world behaves as such, there will be no more purdah.

**Aziz**    It is because you can say and feel such a remark as that, that I show you the photograph. Mr Fielding, no one can ever realise how much kindness we Indians need, we do not even realise it ourselves. But we know when it has been given. Kindness, more kindness, and even after that more kindness. I assure you it is the only hope. (*Pause.*) Put her away, she is of no importance, she is dead. I showed her to you because I have nothing else to show.

**Fielding** *puts the photograph away and sits on the bed. He returns the key to* **Aziz**. **Aziz** *motions to him to replace the key round his neck.* **Fielding** *does.*

**Aziz**   Why are you not married?

**Fielding**   Because I have more or less come through without it. (*Pause.*) The lady I liked wouldn't marry me – that is the main point, but that's fifteen years ago and now means nothing.

**Aziz**   Why don't you marry Miss Quested?

**Fielding**   Good God! Why, the girl's a prig. As it is, I can't marry her if I wanted to, for she has just become engaged to the City Magistrate.

**Aziz**   Has she indeed? I am so glad. Of course, she is not beautiful. She has practically no breasts, if you come to think of it. I shall take you to Calcutta and arrange a lady with breasts like mangoes.

**Fielding**   No you won't . . .

**Aziz**   I suppose now she will be unable to attend the Marabar Caves?

**Fielding**   I fear she is still expecting an invitation. I saw her yesterday on one of my rare visits to the club and she mentioned it.

**Aziz**   Oh, I feel my fever returning. (*He falls back on to his pillows.*)

**Godbole**, *sitting on the carpet, addressing the audience.*

**Godbole**   I miscalculated the length of a prayer. On that day. That particular day. For a moment I was ashamed of religion. Religion can, in a most literal way, make you miss the train. (*Pause.*) But the moment passed.

*A train pulls into the Chandrapore station. Just before dawn. Smoke. Steam. Mist.*

**Aziz** *is huddled in the station, with an ancient cousin of his,* **Mohammed Latif**, *and a group of* **Servants**.

**Mrs Moore**, **Adela** *and their Goanese servant,* **Anthony**, *walk out of the mist.* **Aziz** *rushes to meet them.*

**Aziz**   But you've come after all. Oh, how very kind of you. This is the happiest moment of my life.

**Mrs Moore**   We have so looked forward to this, Dr Aziz.

**Adela**   We're so grateful that you've made the arrangements.

**Aziz**   You come to the carriage and rest until Mr Fielding and the Professor can join us.

**Servants** *are running around with boxes, fruit, towels, a stepladder and a gun.* **Anthony** *watches everything, a smirk on his face.*

**Aziz**   Send back your servant. He is unnecessary. Then we shall all be Moslems together.

**Adela**   And he is such a horrible servant. Anthony, you can go. We don't want you.

**Anthony**   Master told me to come.

**Adela**   Mistress tells you to go.

**Anthony**   Master says keep near the ladies all morning.

**Adela**   Well, your ladies won't have you. Do get rid of him, Dr Aziz.

**Aziz**   Mohammed Latif! Here is my cousin, Mr Mohammed Latif. Oh no, don't shake hands. He is an Indian of the old-fashioned sort, he prefers to salaam.

Mohammed Latif, how beautifully you salaam. See, he
hasn't understood; he knows no English. Isn't he a funny old
man? But you get inside now, make yourselves at home; yes,
you must lie down. Excuse me now, I must meet our other
two guests.

**Aziz** *looks at his watch.* **Mrs Moore** *and* **Adela** *enter their
compartment on the train.*

**Mohammed Latif** *takes out some money and bribes* **Anthony**
*who ultimately leaves the platform.*

**Aziz**, *meanwhile, paces up and down the platform. Suddenly he sees*
**Fielding** *and* **Godbole** *at the level crossing, held up behind a
barricade.*

**Aziz**   Ah, there they are! Mr Fielding! Mr Fielding!

*He shrieks from the pullman carriage. The train has started to move.*

Merciful God!

**Aziz** *and* **Mohammed Latif** *fling themselves on to the train and
leap on to the footground of a carriage.* **Mrs Moore** *and* **Adela** *are
looking out of their compartment window.* **Aziz**, *holding on to a bar,
shouts at them.*

**Aziz**   We're monkeys, don't worry! (*Screams to* **Fielding**
*again.*) Mr Fielding!

*The level crossing bar lifts.* **Fielding** *and* **Godbole** *rush forward.
The train is about to pass them.*

**Aziz** (*shouts to* **Fielding**)   Bad, bad, you have destroyed
me.

**Fielding**   Godbole's prayers did it.

**Aziz**   Jump on, I must have you.

**Fielding**   Right, give me a hand.

**Mrs Moore**   He's not to, he'll kill himself.

**Fielding** *jumps, misses* **Aziz**'s *hand and falls back on to the line.
The train rumbles past.*

**Aziz**   Mrs Moore, Miss Quested, our expedition is a ruin. (*Inches towards their compartment.*)

**Mrs Moore**   Get in, get in, you'll kill yourself as well as Mr Fielding. I see no ruin.

**Aziz**   How is that?

**Mrs Moore**   We shall all be Moslems together, as you promised.

**Aziz** (*smiles*)   Mrs Moore, I would die to make you happy.

**Mrs Moore**   Oh, tosh. Just get in, Dr Aziz, you make us giddy.

**Aziz** *crawls into their compartment, followed by* **Mohammed Latif**.

**Aziz**   Mohammed Latif, what is in these caves, brother? Why are we going to see them?

*The train rides through the dawn. Then it slows alongside an elephant. It stops. A platform is placed leading from the ladies' carriage to the elephant.*

**Aziz**   It takes an hour to get there, an hour to get back, and two hours for the caves. Four hours – quite a small expedition – and an hour extra for misfortunes. If at any point you wish an alteration to the plans, you must tell me and it is done. Do you agree? Then mount this wild animal.

*The elephant kneels. They come up a ladder and mount the elephant. The elephant rises and walks towards the hills. Below the elephant – sounds of villagers, babies, servants. A strange spiritual silence as the elephant moves forward. Then from the hills a brief whisper of* **Godbole***'s song . . .*

**Godbole**   Come, come, come, come . . .

*The whisper fades away.*

*The elephant arrives at a place of stones and rocks and boulders.*

**Aziz**   Do you ever remember our mosque, Mrs Moore?

**Mrs Moore**   I do, I do.

**Aziz**   And how tough and rude I was and how good you were.

**Mrs Moore**   And how happy we both were.

**Aziz**   Friendships last longest that begin like that, I think. Shall I ever entertain your other children?

**Adela**   Do you know about the others? She will never talk about them to me.

**Aziz**   Ralph and Stella, yes, I know everything about them.

*The elephant stops.* **Adela** *and* **Mrs Moore** *are helped down.* **Adela** *suddenly shrieks.*

**Mrs Moore**   What is it?

**Adela** (*points to the ground*)   A snake!

**Aziz**   Yes. It must be a black cobra. Very venomous.

**Adela** *takes out a pair of field glasses and looks through them.*

**Adela**   No. No. It isn't a snake.

**Aziz**   Isn't a snake?

**Adela**   Just a tree stump, I think.

**Aziz**   It's striking, isn't it?

**Mrs Moore** (*quietly, to* **Adela**)   A horrid, stuffy place, I think.

*A* **Servant** *brings them tea.*

**Mrs Moore**   How very well it is all arranged.

**Adela**   You know, Dr Aziz, that I am going to marry Mrs Moore's son.

**Aziz**   Ah, of course – Mr Heaslop. On which my heartfelt congratulations.

**Adela**   Mrs Moore, may I put our difficulty to Dr Aziz – I mean our Anglo-Indian one?

**Mrs Moore**   It is your difficulty, not mine, my dear.

**Adela**   Ah, that's true. Well – by marrying Mr Heaslop I shall become what is known as Anglo-Indian.

**Aziz**   Impossible. Take back such a terrible remark.

**Adela**   But I shall, it's inevitable. I can't avoid the label. What I do hope to avoid is the mentality. Some of the women are so – well, ungenerous and snobby about Indians, and I should feel too ashamed for words if I turned like them, but there's nothing special about me, nothing specially good or strong, which will help me to resist my environment and avoid becoming like them. I've most lamentable defects.

**Aziz**   You are absolutely unlike the others, I assure you. You will never be rude to my people.

**Adela**   I am told we all get rude after a year.

**Aziz**   Then you are told a lie.

**Mrs Moore** *closes her eyes.*

**Aziz**   Come – let us explore the caves.

**Mrs Moore** *opens her eyes.*

**Mrs Moore**   Pardon?

**Aziz**   The caves . . .

**Mrs Moore**   Oh, but surely we can't all go in. We are such a crowd.

**Aziz**   Just villagers. Very friendly.

**Mrs Moore**   And the animals?

**Aziz**   Oh yes. And the babies as well. They are all very proud of their caves.

**Mrs Moore** *smiles but is obviously reluctant to move.*

*They move into the cave.*

**Godbole** *sitting on the carpet, addressing the audience.*

**Godbole**    It is not possible. I will not even try to describe the caves. They are dark, of course. Even when they open towards the sun, very little light penetrates down the entrance tunnel into the circular chamber. There is little to see, and no eye to see it, until the visitor arrives for his five minutes and strikes a match.

**Mrs Moore***'s face: she has entered a cave.*

**Adela** *and* **Aziz** *are there as well. Villagers, babies, animals, servants also. It's as if all of India were in this one small cave. Indeed, it is as if the cave were made out of the people. The cave is dark. We can only see* **Mrs Moore***. Everything, everyone else is in shadow.* **Mrs Moore** *is breathless. She feels faint.*

**Godbole***'s song insinuates itself in the distance, then disappears when* **Aziz** *lights a match, which produces an echo.* **Mrs Moore** *holds her ears. Some naked thing strikes her face. A baby's hand, but she cannot see it. She tries to return to the entrance, but the influx of villagers sweeps her back. She hits her head. For an instance, she goes mad, hitting and gasping like a fanatic. The echo continues. It is devoid of distinction — boom is the sound — but it is terrifying.* **Mrs Moore** *is overwhelmed by sound and smells and humanity; the cave seems to be moving in circles. She is swept back to the entrance. She rushes out of the cave into the sunlight.*

**Mrs Moore** *stands outside the cave, gasping. She looks at the others emerging and realises that none are villains.*

**Adela** *is now standing by her.*

**Adela**    Did you see the reflection of his match? Rather pretty.

**Mrs Moore**    I forgot.

**Adela**    But he says this isn't a good cave, the best are on the other side.

**Mrs Moore**    I don't think I shall go on to there.

**Adela**   Very well, let's sit down again in the shade until breakfast is ready.

**Mrs Moore**   Ah, but that'll disappoint him; he has taken so much trouble. You should go on; I don't mind.

**Adela**   Perhaps I ought to.

**Aziz** *comes to them.*

**Adela**   Mrs Moore wishes to rest a while. She would like us to go ahead without her.

**Aziz**   Certainly, Miss Quested, then you and I will go together.

**Mrs Moore**   Quite right. I'm sorry not to come too but I am a poor walker.

**Aziz**   Dear Mrs Moore, what does anything matter so long as you are my guest. I am very glad that you are not coming, which sounds strange, but you are treating me with true frankness, as a friend.

**Mrs Moore** (*lays her hand on his sleeve tenderly*)   Yes. I am your friend. (*Pause.*) So may I make another suggestion? Don't let so many people with you this time. I think you may find it more convenient.

**Aziz**   Exactly, exactly. (*To* **Servants**.) We will only take one guide with us.

**Mrs Moore**   Quite right. Now, enjoy yourselves, and when you come back, tell me all about it.

*She sinks into a deckchair.* **Aziz**, **Adela** *and a* **Guide** *start off.* **Mrs Moore** *takes out a writing pad and starts to write.*

**Mrs Moore**   Dear Stella, dear Ralph. (*She stops. She looks over at* **Mohammed Latif**.) Did you hear that noise in the cave? There was a sound. Do you understand me? No? Good. Something spoke to me, something very old and very small, something before time, before space also. Did you hear it? Something incapable of generosity. Do you feel despair? Perhaps the despair I feel is only *my* despair, my own personal weakness. After all, if I suddenly got sunstroke and went mad the rest of the world would go on, wouldn't it? (*He smiles at her, uncomprehending.*) I don't want to write to my children. I don't want to commmunicate with anyone, not even God. (*Her words frighten her. She sits motionless with terror.*)

**Aziz**, **Adela** *and the* **Guide** *climb rocks leading to the larger caves.*

**Aziz**    I'm sure we'll find some interesting carvings in the next caves.

**Adela**    Oh yes. I would think so.

**Aziz** *and* **Adela** *voice their inner thoughts, interspersed with their public conversation.*

**Aziz** (*inner thoughts*)    I have very little to say to this woman. I do not like her near as much as Mrs Moore.

**Aziz**    You're not too hot?

**Adela**    No. I'm fine. Thank you.

**Adela** (*inner thoughts*)    I must stop complaining about Anglo-Indians. There is still so much to do. I know there will be difficulties – Ronny's limitations and my own – but I enjoy facing difficulties. I think our married life can be happy and profitable. I mustn't be too theoretical; I'll deal with each problem as it comes up; I'll trust in Ronny's common sense and my own. Luckily we both have an abundance of common sense. (*Pause.*) But what about love? Ronny and I do not love each other.

**Aziz**    Would you like to rest?

**Adela**    No, please let's go on. (*Inner thoughts.*) Ronny and I do not love each other.

**Aziz**    It gets steep here. Take my hand.

**Adela**    Thank you. (*She takes his hand.*)

**Aziz**    Did I take you too fast?

**Adela** (*inner thoughts*)   Not to love the man one's going to marry! Not to find it out until this moment! Not even to have asked oneself the question until now! (*Public.*) No, I'm all right, thanks. (*Inner thoughts.*) Should I break the engagement? It would cause so much trouble to others. Besides, I'm not convinced that love is necessary to a successful union. (*Public.*) Are you married, Dr Aziz?

**Aziz**   Yes indeed.

**Adela**   And have you children?

**Aziz**   Yes indeed. Three.

**Adela**   And they are a great pleasure to you?

**Aziz**   Why, naturally I adore them. (*Inner thoughts.*) I suppose her breasts are sufficient for the City Magistrate.

**Adela** (*inner thoughts*)   What a handsome little Oriental he is.

**Aziz** (*inner thoughts*)   But her face is so plain.

**Adela** (*inner thoughts*)   I suppose he must attract women of his own race.

**Aziz** (*inner thoughts*)   She has no physical charm.

**Adela** (*inner thoughts*)   I have no physical charm. It does make a difference in a relationship – beauty, thick hair, a fine skin. (*Public.*) Have you one wife or more than one?

**Aziz** (*inner thoughts*)   How can she ask that! I am an educated Moslem. How can she ask . . . (*Public.*) One, one in my particular case. (*Lets go of her hand. Inner thoughts.*) Damn the English, even at their best!

**Adela**   We have arrived.

**Aziz**   Yes. We have. One moment, if you please . . .

*Aziz walks off and disappears round a bend. Adela looks ahead of her to the entrance of the caves and then back at the rocks.*

*It is suddenly very hot. She wipes her brow. She hears* **Godbole***'s song in the distance:* 'Come, come, come, come . . .' *She moves towards the entrance of the cave, and then, in a split second, unseen by the* **Guide***, walks into it.*

*She is alone in the cave, enveloped by darkness. She lights a match.*

*A terrifying echo: BOOM!!!!!!!!!!!!!*

*Darkness.*

**Aziz** *sits inside another cave, smoking. He composes himself. He leaves and returns to the rocks where he left* **Adela***. Only the* **Guide** *is there, listening to a noise below.*

**Aziz**  What is that?

**Guide**  Noise.

**Aziz**  It sounds like a motor car. (*Looks down over the rocks.*) Yes, coming towards the hills. Let's tell Miss Quested. (*Pause.*) Where is she?

**Guide**  She goes into the cave.

**Aziz**  Which cave?

**Guide**  One of those.

**Aziz**  What? You should have kept her in sight, it was your duty. Here are twelve caves at least. How am I to know which one contains my guest? Which even is the cave I was in myself? (*Looks at caves and is even unsure which direction he came from.*) Merciful heavens, Miss Quested is lost. Shout. Shout her name. Miss Quested!

**Guide**  Miss Quested!

**Aziz**  Miss Quested!

*Her name echoes through the rocks.* **Aziz** *is sweating. He wipes his head. He goes into one cave. Then another. Nothing.*

Come here. (*The* **Guide** *goes to him.*) This is the end of my career, my guest is lost.

**Aziz** *strikes the* **Guide** *in the face. He starts back towards the rocks, then notices something on the ground. He bends down and picks up* **Adela***'s field glasses.*

**Aziz**   Oh my God! Her field glasses!

*The loud scream of a train whistle! Smoke. Noise.*

*The train platform at Chandrapore.*

**Aziz**, **Mohammed Latif** *and* **Mrs Moore** *enter onto the platform.* **Fielding** *rushes up to meet them.*

**Fielding**   I'm so sorry we missed the train. Godbole's prayers took longer than expected. Where is Miss Quested?

**Aziz**   She went for a spin.

**Ronny** *pushes through the crowd, followed by* **Mr Haq**, *a police officer.*

**Mrs Moore**   Ronny!

**Ronny**   Come away now, Mother. (*Takes her arm.*)

**Mrs Moore**   Dr Aziz, I must thank you . . .

**Ronny**   Instantly, Mother! I insist! (*He forcefully pulls a protesting* **Mrs Moore** *away.* **Mr Haq** *steps forward.*)

**Haq**   Dr Aziz, it is my highly painful duty to arrest you.

**Fielding**   Hello, some mistake.

**Haq**   They are my instructions.

**Fielding**   This is nonsense. On what charge do you arrest him?

**Haq**   I am under instructions not to say. Refer to Inspector McBryde.

**Fielding**   Very well. Come along, Aziz, old man; nothing to fuss about, some blunder.

**Aziz** *sobs. He suddenly tries to bolt.* **Fielding** *pulls him back.*

**Fielding**    Oh, for God's sake . . . Never, never act a criminal.

**Aziz** (*softly*)  My children and my name.

**Fielding**    Nothing of the sort. Put your hat straight and take my arm. I'll see you through.

**Aziz** *takes* **Fielding***'s arm. They are escorted by* **Mr Haq** *who is joined by other* **Policemen**. **Mohammed Latif** *starts to wail. Suddenly* **Haq** *and another* **Policeman** *pry* **Aziz** *away from* **Fielding**.

**Aziz**    Fielding – don't leave me.

*The platform is a madhouse. Passengers and porters in all directions. Steam. The* **Policemen** *carrying* **Aziz** *away.*

*A train whistle blares, and it merges with a woman's scream.* **Adela**. *She is on one side of the stage, hysterical.* **Miss Derek** *is attending her, mopping her brow and painfully picking cactus needles out of her arms and legs.*

*The echo is heard: BOOM!!!!!*

*On the other side of the stage –* **Fielding** *and* **McBryde**, *the Superintendent of Police, in the Police Station.*

**McBryde**    All natives are criminals at heart, for the simple reason that they live south of latitude 30. They are not to blame, they have not a dog's chance – we should be like them if we settled here.

**Fielding**    For God's sake, McBryde, what on earth has happened?

**McBryde**    I'm afraid Miss Quested has been insulted in one of the Marabar Caves.

**Fielding**    Oh no, oh no, no, no.

**McBryde**    She escaped by God's grace. Although she is poorly.

**Fielding**   Oh no, no, but not Aziz . . . not Aziz . . .
(**McBryde** *nods.*) What is the charge, precisely?

**McBryde**   That he followed her into the cave and made
insulting advances. She hit at him with her field glasses, he
pulled at them and the strap broke, and that is how she got
away. When we searched him just now they were in his
pocket. I couldn't worry her overmuch with questions. She
is in a shocking state. There was an echo that appears to
have frightened her. Major Callender is very concerned
about her health. Her entire body has been punctured by
cactus needles. Utterly barbaric. I heard some more from
Miss Derek. She heard stones falling and saw Miss Quested
running straight down the face of a precipice. Well. She
climbed up a sort of gully to her and found her practically
done for. She had got among the cactuses. Miss Derek saved
her life coming just then . . .

**Fielding**   I believe Miss Quested must be under some
hideous delusion and that the wretched boy is innocent.

**McBryde**   I had no idea that was in your mind.

**Fielding**   Those field glasses upset me for a minute, but
I've thought since: it's impossible that, having attempted to
assault her, he would put her glasses into his pocket.

**McBryde**   Quite possible, I'm afraid; when an Indian
goes bad, he goes not only very bad, but very queer. The
Lord help us, the Lord help us all.

**Major Callender** *gives* **Adela** *an injection, as* **Miss Derek**
*watches.*

**Fielding** *and* **Godbole** *at* **Fielding**'s *house.*

**Godbole**   Ah, Mr Fielding, I am pleased to find you.
I have an interesting proposition for you to ponder.

**Fielding**   I see the news has not reached you yet.

**Godbole**   Oh yes.

**Fielding**  No: there has been a terrible catastrophe about Aziz.

**Godbole**  Oh yes. That is all round the college.

**Fielding**  I am most frightfully cut up.

**Godbole**  So I saw at once on entering your office. I must not detain you, but I have a small private difficulty on which I want your help: I am leaving your service shortly as you know. And am returning to my birthplace, Mau, in Central India. I want to start a high school there on sound English lines, but the point on which I desire your help is this – what name should be given to the school?

**Fielding**  (*feeling slightly ill*)  A name? A name for a school?

**Godbole**  Yes, a name, a suitable title, by which it can be called.

**Fielding**  Really – I have no names for schools in my head. I can think of nothing but poor Aziz. Have you grasped that at the present moment he is in prison?

**Godbole**  Oh yes. Oh no, I do not expect an answer to my question now. I had thought of the Mr Fielding High School, but failing that King Emperor the Fifth.

**Fielding**  Godbole! (**Godbole** *puts his hands together.*) Is Aziz innocent or guilty?

**Godbole**  That is for the court to decide. The verdict will be in strict accordance with the evidence. I make no doubt.

**Fielding**  Yes, yes, but your personal opinion. Would he or would he not do such a thing?

**Godbole**  Ah. A complicated question. (*Pause.*) The tragedy, of course, is that you missed the interesting Marabar antiquities.

**Fielding** *groans*.

**Adela** *sits up in bed now, staring vacantly into space. She remains there for the rest of the act.*

**Fielding** *walks through the bazaar. A tiger jumps out of the darkness. But it is only a youth dressed up as a tiger, the body striped brown and yellow, a mask over his face. The Festival of Mohurram is beginning. There are drummers on all sides. The drumming is good-natured.* **Fielding** *continues on his way.*

*The club. Drumming is heard in the distance.* **Turton** *addresses* **Mrs Turton** *and a group of* **Englishwomen**. *A young* **Subaltern** *is also present, as well as several other club members, including* **Mr Burton**.

**Turton**    Not the least cause for alarm. Keep cool, keep cool. Don't go out more than you can help, don't go into the city, don't talk before your servants. That's all.

**Mrs Turton**    Harry, is there any news from the city?

**Turton**    Everything absolutely normal.

**Mrs Turton**    Mr McBryde's down there disguised as a Holy Man.

**Turton**    That's exactly the sort of thing that must not be said, Mary, be more careful than that, please. We must not say anything that will cause alarm . . . Are there any questions?

**Englishwoman** (**Mrs Blakiston**)    What if the niggers attack?

**Turton**    They won't, Mrs Blakiston, and anyhow, they're not coming to the club.

**Mrs Turton**    But those drums . . .

**Turton**    Merely Mohurram. Some kind of festival. No need to worry. We have everything well in hand. Will all the ladies leave the smoking room now, please? And remember what I have said. You can help us by behaving as if everything is normal. Can I rely on you?

**Ladies**    Yes indeed . . . Oh indeed . . .

*The* **Ladies** *leave.* **Fielding** *had slipped into the room during their talk. The* **Subaltern** *glares at him.*

**Turton**    Don't go carrying arms about. I want everything to proceed as usual, until there's cause for the contrary. Get the womenfolk off to the hills, but do it quietly.

**Subaltern**    Exactly what I said.

**Burton**    This nonsense would never have happened if we were under military control.

**Turton** (*stares at him, coldly*)    Soldiers put one thing straight, but leave a dozen others crooked.

**Major Callender** *enters.*

**Turton**    Major Callender, how is your patient?

**Callender**    No one's out of danger in this country as long as they have a temperature.

**Turton**    How's the old lady?

**Callender**    Temperature.

**Turton**    My wife heard she was sinking.

**Callender**    I guarantee nothing. I really can't be plagued with questions. I wish to God I hadn't given my assistant leave. I'd cut my tongue out first. To feel I'm responsible; that's what hits me.

**Turton**    No one blames you, my dear Callender.

**Callender**    Heaslop found out something from his mother. Aziz paid a herd of natives to suffocate her in a cave. That was the end of her, or would have been, only she got out. Nicely planned, wasn't it? Then he could go with the girl. He and she and a guide, only the guide now can't be found. Pretty. It's time for action. Call in the troops and clear the bazaars.

**Turton** *clears his throat, makes a hand motion to calm things down.*
**Ronny** *enters, looking exhausted and tragic. The others, in instinctive
homage, rise to their feet.* **Fielding** *remains seated.*

**Ronny**    Oh please, please, all sit down. I only wanted to
listen to what has been decided.

**Turton**    Heaslop, I'm telling them I'm against any show
of force. When the verdict is obtained, it will be another
matter.

**Ronny**    You are sure to know best.

**Turton**    How is your mother, old boy?

**Ronny**    Better, thank you. I wish everyone would sit
down.

**Subaltern**    Some have never got up.

**Turton**    Mr Fielding, what has prevented you from
standing up?

**Fielding**    May I make a statement, sir?

**Turton**    Certainly.

**Fielding** (*rises*)    I believe Dr Aziz to be innocent.

**Turton**    You have a right to hold that opinion if you
choose, but is that any reason why you should insult Mr
Heaslop?

**Fielding**    May I conclude my statement?

**Turton**    Certainly.

**Fielding**    I am waiting for the court. If he is guilty I resign
from my service and leave India. I resign from the club.

**Members**    Hear, hear.

**Turton**    You have not answered my question. Why did
you not stand when Mr Heaslop entered?

**Fielding**    With all deference, sir, I am not here to answer questions but to make a personal statement and I have concluded it.

**Turton**    One moment, Mr Fielding. You are not to go yet, please. Before you leave the club, from which you do very well to resign, will you express some detestation of the crime and will you apologise to Mr Heaslop?

**Fielding**    Are you speaking to me officially, sir?

**Turton** (*infuriated*)    Leave this room at once. You have sunk to the level of your associates.

**Fielding** *tries to reach the door but the* **Subaltern** *stands in his path, blocking him.*

**Fielding**    I want to leave the room but cannot while this gentleman prevents me.

**Ronny**    Let him go.

*The* **Subaltern** *moves aside reluctantly.* **Fielding** *walks out.*

**Turton**    I'm afraid Mr Fielding has long been a disruptive force. If you remember he remarked last year that the white races are in fact really pinko-grey. Mrs Turton picked up on that at once. I tried to give the fellow a chance. After all, I don't believe in rushing to judgement.

**Adela**'s *eyes open wide. She starts to sit up, then falls back on the bed.*

**Aziz** *is in a prison cell. A* **Guard** *opens the door.* **Fielding** *walks in.*

**Aziz**    Cyril, why did you desert me?

**Fielding**    I did not desert you.

**Aziz**    I thought you would not come.

**Fielding**    I am here now. I am here.

*They reach out to each other – and grasp their hands together.*

**Godbole** *enters*.

**Godbole**    Tonight when our ceremony begins and our
God is born, infinite love will take the form of Shri Krishna
and save the world. All sorrow will disappear, not only for
Indians, but for foreigners, birds, caves, railways and the
stars. All will become joy and laughter, there will have been
no disease, no doubt, misunderstanding, cruelty, fear. It
happens in a moment, and then . . . once we have thought
we were with God, that moment becomes history and
disappears.

# Act Two

*Mau.* **Professor Godbole**, *barefoot and in white, addresses the audience.*

**Godbole**  You ask about the Marabar Caves. You ask what happened. You ask about the 'mystery'. What you want to know is: did our friend Dr Aziz commit an evil action. Assuming an action, any action, was committed. Would you like me to answer? Ah, but the question is a difficult one in our philosophy. It presumes that an individual can commit good actions or evil actions. Difficult. Because nothing can be performed in isolation. All perform a good action, when one is performed, and when an evil action is performed, all perform it. To illustrate my meaning let me take the case in point as an example. My answer is this: if such an action was performed, it was performed by Dr Aziz. (*Pause.*) It was performed by the guide. (*Pause.*) It was performed by me. It was performed by you. And by my students. It was even performed by the lady herself. Does that solve the 'mystery' for you? You see, when evil occurs, it expresses the whole of the universe. Similarly when good occurs. Good and evil are not what we think them, they are both what they are, and each of us has contributed to them both. Perhaps you ask then are good and evil the same? Oh no, you must not think that. Good and evil are different, as their names imply. But in my own humble opinion they are both of them aspects of my Lord. He is present in the one, absent in the other, and the difference between presence and absence is great. Yet absence implies presence, absence is not nonexistence, and we are therefore entitled to repeat 'Come, come, come, come . . .' (*Pause.*) I hope that answers your questions. Now the holy festival is to begin. Our God is soon to be born. And the Sweepers Band will soon arrive. Our God, once born, cannot leave his temple until the unclean sweepers play their tune. It takes a spot of filth, after all, for the spirit to cohere.

*The mist returns and Mau disappears.*

*Chandrapore.* **Aziz** *walks through the mist.* **Indians** *surround him, shouting. They begin to riot. They throw rocks, break windows.* **Aziz** *is swallowed up by the crowd.*

**Adela** *sits in a chair – on the other side of the stage. She is dressed.* **Miss Derek** *attends her. Noises of the rioting can be heard outside.*

**Adela**    I went into this detestable cave . . .

**Miss Derek**    There's no need to go through it again . . .

**Adela**    And I remember scratching the wall with my fingernail . . .

*On the other side of the stage – a prison cell.* **Fielding** *visiting* **Aziz***.*

**Aziz**    Two hours!

**Fielding**    You were free for two hours?

**Aziz**    Yes. On bail. But as soon as they released me the riots started. So they returned me to prison and honoured me with an additonal charge: disturbing the public peace.

**Fielding**    I brought you some mangoes.

**Adela** *is continuing her tale.*

**Adela**    . . . and then as I was saying there was this shadow, or sort of shadow, down the entrance tunnel, bottling me up. It seemed like an age, but I suppose the whole thing can't have lasted thirty seconds really. I hit at him with the glasses, he pulled me round the cave by the strap, it broke, I escaped, that's all. He never actually touched me once. It all seems such nonsense.

**Miss Derek**    My dear . . .

**Adela**    You've been so kind to me. How can I ever repay you? How can one repay when one has nothing to give? I'm not fit for personal relationships – of any kind.

**Miss Derek** *(touches her arm)*    My dear . . .

**Adela**   No, no, don't touch me – please.

*The prison cell.*

**Aziz**   Do you know who my favourite emperor is? Not Alamgir, as you might imagine. No, it is Babar. Not a pious man, like Alamgir. And you know how he died? He laid down his life for his son. They were caught in the desert heat. His son fell sick. Babar walked round his son's bed three times and said, 'I have borne it away,' and he did bear it away; the fever left his son and came to him instead, and he died. This is why I prefer Babar to Alamgir. (*He takes the mangoes from* **Fielding**.)

**Ronny**'s *bungalow.* **Mrs Moore** *sits on a sofa, looking at a list of steamship sailings.* **Ronny** *enters with a very fragile* **Adela**. **Mrs Moore** *does not get up.*

**Mrs Moore**   Here you are both back.

**Adela** *sits down and takes* **Mrs Moore**'s *hand.* **Mrs Moore** *withdraws it.*

**Ronny**   Are you all right? You appeared all right when I left.

**Mrs Moore**   I am all right. As a matter of fact I have been looking at my return ticket. It is interchangeable so I have a much larger choice of boats home than I thought.

**Ronny**   We can go into that later, can't we?

**Mrs Moore**   Ralph and Stella may be wanting to know when I arrive.

**Ronny**   There is plenty of time for all such plans. How do you think our Adela looks?

**Adela** (*to* **Mrs Moore**)   I am counting on you to help me through; it is such a blessing to be with you again. These past two weeks at the McBrydes were very difficult; I was, of course – well – feverish for some of the time and they were all so kind, but still, they were strangers. I know it's all nothing; I must be sensible, I do try – but there is this echo that I keep on hearing.

**Mrs Moore**   Oh, what of the echo?

**Adela**   I can't get rid of it.

**Mrs Moore**   I don't suppose you ever will.

**Adela**   Mrs Moore, what is this echo?

**Mrs Moore**   Don't you know?

**Adela**   No, what is it? Oh, do say! I felt you would be able to explain it.

**Mrs Moore**   If you don't know, you don't know; I can't tell you.

**Adela**   I think you're rather unkind not to say.

**Mrs Moore**   Say, say, say. As if anything can be said! I have spent my life in saying or in listening to sayings! I have listened too much. It is time I was left in peace. Not to die. No doubt you expect me to die, but when I have seen you and Ronny married and seen the other two and whether they want to be married – I'll retire into a cave of my own. (*Smiles.*) Somewhere where no young people will come asking questions and expecting answers. Some shelf.

**Ronny**   Quite so, but meantime a trial is coming up. (*To* **Adela**.) The case will come before Das, my assistant. He's intelligent and of course can only come to one conclusion. Still, the notion of most of us is that we'd better pull together and help one another through, instead of . . . (*Looks at* **Mrs Moore**.) being disagreeable. Are you going to talk like that in the witness box?

**Mrs Moore**   Why should I be in the witness box?

**Ronny**   To confirm certain points in our evidence.

**Mrs Moore**   I have nothing to do with your ludicrous law courts. I will not be dragged in at all.

**Adela**   I won't have her dragged in either. I won't have any more trouble on my account. (*Takes* **Mrs Moore***'s hand, which is again withdrawn.*) Her evidence is not the least essential.

**Ronny**   I thought she would want to give it. No one blames you, Mother, but the fact remains that you dropped off at the first cave, and encouraged Adela to go on with him alone, whereas if you'd been well enough to keep on too, nothing would have happened. Forgive me for speaking so plainly but you've no right to take up this high and mighty attitude about law courts. I thought you would want to take your part; I really did.

**Mrs Moore**   I shall attend your marriage, but not your trial. Then I shall go to England.

**Ronny**   You can't go to England in May. We agreed.

**Mrs Moore**   I have changed my mind.

**Ronny**   You appear to want to be left out of everything.

**Mrs Moore**   My body, my miserable body. Why isn't it strong? Oh, why can't I walk away and be gone? Why can't I finish my duties and be gone? Why do I get headaches and puff when I walk? And all the time this to do in her way and that to do in your way, and everything sympathy and confusion and bearing one another's burdens. Why can't this be done and that be done in my way and they be done and I at peace? Why has anything to be done, I cannot see. Why all this marriage, marriage? . . . The human race would have become a single person centuries ago if marriage was any use. And all this rubbish about love, love in a church, love in a cave, as if there is the least difference, and I held up from my business over such trifles!

**Ronny**   What do you want? Can you state it in simple language? If so, do.

**Mrs Moore**   I want my pack of patience cards.

**Ronny**   Very well, get them.

**Mrs Moore** *rises and walks out of the room.* **Adela** *starts to weep.*

**Ronny**   Well, my dear girl, this isn't much of a homecoming. I had no idea she had this up her sleeve.

**Adela** *stops crying. She looks both relieved and horrified.*

**Adela**   Aziz, Aziz . . .

**Ronny**   What the dickens? . . .

**Adela**   Aziz . . . have I made a mistake?

**Ronny**   You're overtired.

**Adela**   Ronny, he's innocent; I made an awful mistake.

**Ronny**   Sit down . . . please . . .

*They sit. She takes his hand and strokes it and smiles, then gasps and touches her ear.*

**Adela**   My echo's better.

**Ronny**   That's good. You'll be perfectly well in a few days, but you must save yourself up for the trial.

**Adela**   But Ronny, Ronny dear, perhaps there oughtn't to be any trial.

**Ronny**   I don't quite know what you're saying, and I don't think you do.

**Adela**   If Dr Aziz never did it he ought to be let out. (*Clings to him.*) Help me to do what I ought. Aziz is good. You heard your mother say so.

**Ronny**   Heard what?

**Adela**   He's good; I've been so wrong to accuse him.

**Ronny**   Mother never said so.

**Adela**   Didn't she?

**Ronny**   She never mentioned the name once.

**Adela**    But Ronny, I heard her.

**Ronny**    Pure illusion. You can't be quite well, can you, to make up a thing like that?

**Adela**    I suppose I can't. How amazing of me.

**Ronny**    I was listening to all she said, as far as it could be listened to: she gets very incoherent.

**Adela**    When her voice dropped she said it – towards the end, when she talked about love – love – I couldn't follow, but just then she said, 'Dr Aziz never did it.'

**Ronny**    Those words?

**Adela**    The idea more than the words.

**Ronny**    Never, never, my dear girl. His name was not mentioned by anyone. So you won't go on saying he's innocent again, will you? For every servant I've got is a spy.

**Mrs Moore** *returns with her patience cards and sits at the card table.*

**Ronny**    Mother, did you mention the prisoner's name?

**Mrs Moore**    I don't understand the question.

**Ronny**    Adela thought she heard you say the prisoner's name.

**Mrs Moore**    I never said his name. (*Begins to play patience.*)

**Adela**    I thought you said, 'Aziz is an innocent man.'

**Mrs Moore**    Of course he is innocent.

**Adela**    You see, Ronny, I was right.

**Ronny**    You were not right, she never said it.

**Adela** · But she thinks it.

**Ronny**    Who cares what she thinks.

**Mrs Moore** ( *from the card table*)    Red nine on black ten.

**Ronny**   She can think whatever she wants, but there's such a thing as evidence, I suppose.

**Adela**   I know, but –

**Mrs Moore**   Is it again my duty to talk? Apparently, as you keep interrupting me.

**Ronny**   Only if you have anything sensible to say.

**Mrs Moore**   Oh, why is everything still my duty? When shall I be free from your fuss? Was he in the cave and were you in the cave and on and on. . . and unto us a son is born, unto us a child is given . . . and am I glad and is he bad and are we saved? . . . and ending everything, the echo.

**Adela**   I don't hear it so much. You send it away, you do nothing but good, you are good.

**Mrs Moore**   I am not good, no, bad. (*Returns to her cards.*) A bad old woman, bad, bad, detestable. I used to be good with the children growing up. Also I met the young man in his mosque, I wanted him to be happy. Good, happy, small people. They don't exist, they were a dream. But I will not help you to torture him for what he never did. Nothing happened, and if it had, there are worse evils than love.

**Ronny**   Have you any evidence in the prisoner's favour? If so, it is your bounded duty to go into the witness box for him instead of for us. No one will stop you.

**Mrs Moore**   One knows people's characters, as you call them. I feel it isn't the sort of thing he would do.

**Ronny**   Feeble, Mother, feeble.

**Mrs Moore**   Most feeble.

**Ronny**   And most inconsiderate to Adela.

**Adela**   It would be so appalling if I was wrong. I should take my own life.

**Ronny**   What was I warning you just now? You know you're right, and the whole station knows it.

**Adela**   Yes, he . . . This is very very awful. I'm as certain as ever he followed me . . . only wouldn't it be possible to withdraw the case? I dread the idea of giving evidence more and more . . . Oh, of course, it's out of the question, I'm ashamed to have mentioned it; please forgive me.

**Ronny**   That's all right. The case has to come before a magistrate now; it really must, the machinery has started.

**Mrs Moore**   She has started the machinery; it will work to its end.

**Ronny** (*stares at her*)   Perhaps you're right, Mother. Perhaps you should leave India at once. (*He picks up the list of steamship sailings.*)

*A prison cell.* **Aziz** *is with* **Fielding**, **Hamidullah** *and* **Rafi**.

**Rafi**   The sweepers are on strike, and remain so until you are acquitted.

**Hamidullah**   A number of Mohammedan Indians have sworn to take no food until you are acquitted.

**Aziz**   Their death will make little difference.

**Fielding**   Why do you say so, my friend?

**Aziz**   Because it has been decided already. Has it not? It is fate!

*The others look at him and cannot speak.*

*A* **Young Man**, *almost naked, sits on a raised platform and pulls a punkah – a large fixed and swinging fan, formed of cloth, stretched on a rectangular frame, suspended from the ceiling.*

*It is the courtroom.*

*The assistant magistrate,* **Das**, *cultivated, self-conscious and conscientious, sits on a platform in the centre.* **Ronny**, **Adela**, **Mrs Turton** *and* **Major Callender** *enter on one side. They are joined by* **McBryde** *who will be prosecuting. On the other side, a pale and nervous* **Aziz**, *flanked by his legal team,* **Mahmoud Ali** *and a fine-looking barrister from Calcutta,* **Amritrao**. **Fielding**

*enters the courtroom. There is a frisson as he takes a seat next to the
Indians. He does not look at the British.*

**Adela** *and* **Aziz** *turn and stare at each other. Suddenly* **Godbole**'s
*song is heard and everyone fades from view, except for* **Adela** *and*
**Aziz**, *who are both pinpointed in isolated lights. They can only see
each other. They are surrounded by shadows — shadows of their friends,
shadows of the courtroom — and sound — the sound of the punkah and
fluttering fans in the hands of the female spectators. The sounds of
people gossiping and coughing. And the sound of the echo in* **Adela**'s
*head. People try to crowd into their light, but we only see the outer edges
of bodies. Voices merge into one another.*

**Das**   Order, order . . .

**Ronny**   I've given Das good training; he'll be all right. . .

**Mrs Turton**   Not one of them's all right.

**Ronny**   Das is, really.

**Hamidullah**   We are lucky. Mr Amritrao is a Calcutta
barrister with a high professional reputation.

**Fielding**   And notoriously anti-British. Aziz must be
cleared with the minimum of racial hatred.

**Hamidullah**   Oh no, we must hit with all our strength.

**Fielding**   We're bound to win. She will never be able to
substantiate the charge.

**Mrs Turton**   You mean your Das is more frightened of
acquitting than convicting because if he acquits he will lose
his job.

**Ronny**   Conviction is inevitable; so better let an Indian
pronounce it.

**Das**   Order! Superintendent McBryde, you may begin.

**McBryde**'s *shadow looms over* **Aziz**.

**McBryde**   This man before us, this Dr Aziz, is guilty of a
most heinous crime. Everyone knows this to be true, and I

am obliged to say so in public. The darker races are physically attracted by the fairer, but not vice versa – not a matter of bitterness this, not a matter for abuse, but just a fact which any scientific observer will confirm.

**Voice**   Even when the lady is uglier than the gentleman?

**Das**   Turn that man out! If there are any other comments I will clear the gallery.

**Mrs Turton**   Do you feel faint, Miss Quested?

**Adela**   I never feel anything else.

**Major Callender**   Really, old man, better arrangements should be made for Miss Quested. She gets no air. Why isn't she given a seat on the platform?

**Das**   I shall be happy to accommodate Miss Quested with a chair up here in view of the particular circumstances of her health.

*The bustle of chairs raised on to the platform.* **Adela**, *pinpointed in her light, moves on to the platform; pieces of chairs are thrust into her light. We can sense that the entire British party has followed* **Adela** *on to the platform.*

**Mrs Turton**   That's better.

**Major Callender**   Right, McBryde, go ahead now; sorry to have interrupted you.

**McBryde**   We will also show that the prisoner is a man of loose life, as photographs found upon him at his arrest will testify . . .

**Mahmoud Ali**   May I ask why my client cannot be accommodated on the platform too; even Indians feel unwell sometimes.

**Das**   Mr Mahmoud Ali, please take your seat. Mr Amritrao?

**Amritrao**   Excuse me. We object to the presence of so many European ladies and gentlemen upon the platform.

They will have the effect of intimidating our witnesses.
Their place is with the rest of the people in the body of the
hall. We have no objection to Miss Quested remaining on
the platform since she has been unwell; we shall extend
every courtesy to her throughout.

**Mrs Turton**    I do wish he would just give the verdict.

**Das**    It was only to Miss Quested that I gave permission to
sit up here. Her friends should be excessively kind to climb
down.

**Ronny**    Well done, Das, quite sound.

**Mrs Turton**    Climb down, indeed, what incredible
impertinence.

**Major Callender**    All this moving around is unhealthy in
this heat.

*The clatter of chairs descending from the platform, along with* **Adela**,
*as her light shifts with her. A cheer is raised in the gallery.* **Das** *bangs
for silence.*

**Das**    Mr McBryde . . .

**McBryde**    Yes. I would like to deal at length with the
prisoner's dupes and indeed, to show a plan of the Marabar
Hills, where this dreadful deed took place . . .

*On the side of the stage – a carriage on a mail train.* **Mrs Moore** *is
writing a letter.*

**Mrs Moore**    I suppose I have all I wished for. I have
escaped the trial, the marriage and the hot weather, and
soon I will see you, dearest Ralph and Stella, but that and
that alone fills me with enthusiasm. I'm afraid I have
reached a state where the horror of the universe and its
smallness are both visible at the same time – what can I call
it? – it's a sort of twilight of the double vision in which so
many elderly people like myself are involved. If this world is
not to my taste, well, at all events there is Heaven, Hell,
Annihilation – one or other of those large things, that huge

scenic background of stars, fires, blue or black air. But in this twilight of the double vision a spiritual muddledom is set up for which no high-sounding word can be found; we can neither act nor refrain from action, we can neither ignore nor respect infinity. Oh, wouldn't it be simple – not to mention dignified – if one could be one with the universe. Ah yes. Indeed. I hesitate sometimes putting my thoughts to you, but there is something of me in the two of you, I know that, whereas I seem to be entirely absent from your half-brother.

*The courtroom. The two lights persisting on* **Adela** *and* **Aziz**.

**McBryde** *is in mid-speech.*

**McBryde**   . . . and finally, the culminating evidence: the discovery of the field glasses on the prisoner. The prisoner is one of those individuals who have led a double life. He has been very cunning at concealing and pretending to be a respectable member of society, getting a government position even. He behaved most cruelly, brutally, to another of his guests, another English lady. In order to get rid of her and leave him free for his crime, he crushed her into a cave, among his servants. However, that is by the by . . .

**Mahmoud Ali**   Is my client charged with murder as well as rape?

**Das**   Mr Mahmoud Ali . . .

**Mahmoud Ali**   Who is this second English lady?

**McBryde**   I don't propose to call her.

**Mahmoud Ali**   You don't because you can't, you have smuggled her out of the country; she is Mrs Moore, she would have proved his innocence, she was on our side, she was the poor Indian's friend.

**Das**   You could have called her yourself. Neither side called her; neither must quote her as evidence.

**Mahmoud Ali**    She was kept from us until too late – I learn too late – this is British justice, here is your British Raj. Give us back Mrs Moore for five minutes only and she will save my friend; tell me where they have put her . . .

**Ronny**    If the point is of any interest, my mother should be reaching Aden . . .

**Mahmoud Ali**    Imprisoned by you there because she knew the truth!

*The carriage on the mail train.* **Mrs Moore** *continues her letter.*

**Mrs Moore**    In the morning I shall reach the boat. Meanwhile, we have passed a place called Asirgarh. I have never heard of it. It had large and noble bastions, and to the right of them was a mosque. And then, ten minutes later, Asirgarh reappeared. The mosque was to the left of the bastions now. The train in its descent has described a semicircle around Asirgarh. I know no one who lives there and nothing about it, but it looked at me twice and seemed to say 'I do not vanish'.

*The courtroom. There is tumult from the gallery.*

**Mahmoud Ali**    I ruin my career; no matter; we are all to be ruined, one by one.

**Das**    This is no way to defend your case.

**Mahmoud Ali**    I am not defending a case, nor are you trying one. We are both of us slaves . . .

**Das**    Mr Mahmoud Ali, I have already warned you, and unless you sit down, I shall exercise my authority.

**Mahmoud Ali**    Do so; this trial is a farce, I am going! (*The sound of* **Mahmoud Ali** *handing his papers to* **Amritrao** *and walking away, calling from the doorway.*) Aziz, Aziz – farewell for ever!

**Aziz**, *in his spotlight, squirms. The tumult increases. The name 'Mrs Moore' is shouted outside the courtroom by the crowd, but they pronounce it Esmiss Esmoor.*

**Mrs Turton**    What are they saying?

**Major Callender**    Mrs Moore, I think.  Most
unexpected.

**Mrs Turton**    Mr Heaslop, how disgraceful, dragging in
your dear mother.

**Crowd** (*outside the courtroom*)    Esmiss Esmoor, Esmiss
Esmoor, Esmiss Esmoor . . .

**Adela**    Ronny?

**Ronny** (*his face intrudes into her light*)    Is it very upsetting for
you?

**Adela**    Not in the least. I don't mind it.

**Ronny**    Well, that's good.

**Adela**    Don't worry about me. I'm much better than I
was. I don't feel in the least faint.

*Suddenly the chanting stops.*

**Das**    Mr McBryde, were you to call witnesses?

**McBryde**    Yes. I would ask Miss Quested to please give
evidence.

**Adela** *hesitates.* **Ronny**'s *hand extends into her light and grips her
hand. She walks on to the platform and sits in the witness chair.*

**McBryde**    Miss Quested, I will try not to prolong your
ordeal. Was my description of Dr Aziz invitation correct?

**Adela**    Yes, he invited us to see the caves.

**McBryde**    And on the day, did you and Mrs Moore make
the expedition with him alone, due to the sudden absence of
Mr Fielding and Professor Godbole.

**Adela**    Yes. We did.

**McBryde**    An elephant met you at the train?

**Adela**    Yes. It did.

**McBryde**   And a crowd of people?

**Adela**   Yes.

**McBryde**   And you arrived at the caves?

**Adela**   Yes.

**McBryde**   And how did you find the expedition?

**Adela**   Rather dull, actually. (*Pause.*) Disappointing. In the first cave, a match was reflected in the polished walls. That was rather beautiful.

**McBryde**   Was that the cave that tired Mrs Moore?

**Adela**   Yes.

**McBryde**   And she excused herself from further explorations?

**Adela**   Yes.

**McBryde**   And you went then along the rocks . . .

**Adela**   Yes.

**McBryde**   With Dr Aziz and a guide?

**Adela**   Yes.

**McBryde**   To see the larger caves?

**Adela**   Yes.

**McBryde**   And no one else was present?

**Adela**   No. (*Pause.*) No one else was present to my knowledge. We appeared to be alone.

**McBryde**   Very well, there is a ledge halfway up the hill, with caves scattered near the beginning of a watercourse . . .

**Adela**   I know where you mean.

**McBryde**   You went alone into one of those caves.

**Adela**   This is quite correct.

**McBryde**    And the prisoner followed you.

*She is silent.*

The prisoner followed you, didn't he?

**Adela**    May I have half a minute before I reply to that, Mr McBryde?

**McBryde**    Certainly.

*Pause.*

**Adela**    I am not . . . I am not quite sure.

**McBryde**    I beg your pardon?

**Adela**    I cannot be sure.

**McBryde**    I didn't catch that answer. You are on that landing, or whatever we term it, and you have entered a cave. I suggest to you that the prisoner followed you.

*She shakes her head.*

What do you mean, please?

**Adela**    No.

**Das**    What is that? What are you saying?

**Adela**    I'm afraid I have made a mistake.

**Das**    What nature of mistake?

**Adela**    Dr Aziz never followed me into the cave.

**McBryde** (*slams down his papers, then picks them up*)    Now, Miss Quested, let us go on. I will read you the words of the deposition which you signed two hours later in my bungalow . . .

**Das**    Excuse me, Mr McBryde, you cannot go on. I am speaking to the witness myself. And the public will be silent. If it continues to talk, I will have the court cleared. Miss Quested, address your remarks to me, and remember you speak on oath.

**Adela**    Dr Aziz never –

**Major Callender**    I suggest these proceedings be stopped on medical grounds.

*The shadows – of the* **English** *and the* **Indians** *– now loom tall. Everyone has risen in the courtroom. There is a feeling of chaos, a sense that the whole room might explode.*

**Das**    You withdraw the charge? Answer me!

**Adela**    I withdraw everything.

**Das**    Mr McBryde, do you wish to continue in the face of this?

**McBryde** (*to* **Adela**)    Are you mad?

**Das**    Don't question her, sir, you no longer have the right.

**McBryde**    Give me time to consider –

**Amritrao**    You have no choice but to withdraw, lest this becomes a scandal.

**Mrs Turton**    He shall not. Call the other witnesses. We're none of us safe. (*She forces her way into* **Adela**'s *light.*) You stupid bitch!

*Hands pull her back. The chaos has increased. Shadows and sounds are falling over one another.*

**McBryde** (*trying to sound nonchalant*)    Right, I withdraw.

*Shouts and screams from the gallery.* **Das** *pounds his gavel down. Silence.*

**Das**    The prisoner is released without one stain on his character; the question of costs will be decided elsewhere.

*Pandemonium. Suddenly the entire courtroom is brightly lit.*

**Das** *leaves.* **Callender** *restrains* **Mrs Turton** *from lunging at* **Adela**. **Ronny** *is swept up and away by the* **English**. **Aziz** *rises.* **Rafi** *rushes in, jubilant.* **Aziz** *swoons and is caught by* **Rafi**. *He is then lifted high on the shoulders of his friends. Jubilant*

**Townspeople** *run to and fro. Banners appear. Flowers are thrown.* **Fielding** *is celebrating with* **Aziz**, *who now has a garland of jasmine round his neck.*

*By stark contrast,* **Adela** *sits alone in her chair, on the other side of the courtroom in a daze.* **Fielding** *notices her and goes to her. The* **English** *have now totally disappeared.*

**Fielding**    Where will you go, Miss Quested?

**Adela**    I don't know.

**Fielding**    You can't wander about outside.

**Adela**    I shall walk . . .

**Fielding**    What madness. There's a riot on. Why don't you join your own people?

**Adela**    Ought I?

**Fielding**    You can't, it's too late, they've left. Come with me – quick – I'll put you in my carriage.

*He pulls her up from the chair.* **Aziz** *sees him and shouts to him.*

**Aziz**    Cyril, Cyril, don't leave me.

**Fielding**    I'm coming back.

**Aziz**    Cyril . . .

**Fielding** *hurries* **Adela** *out of the room.* **Aziz** *is engulfed by* **Friends** *and* **Wellwishers**. *They carry him out of the room.*

*The courtroom is empty. Only the* **Young Man** *remains, still pulling the punkah, as if nothing has happened.*

*Lights rise on* **Godbole**, *sitting on the carpet.*

*A* **Brahman** *brings a model made of clay and places it on an altar. Clay figures stand on the model – a king and advisers and also the mother and father of the Lord.*

*A cobra of papier mâché appears on the carpet. Also a wooden cradle swinging from a frame.* **Godbole** *approaches the cradle with a red silk napkin in his arms. He turns to the audience.*

**Godbole** The napkin is God. Not that it is. Perhaps you would like me to explain. (*He turns back to the cradle. He folds the napkin into a shape which indicates a baby. He places the napkin in the cradle.*) Ah – but has a mud village or a silk napkin or an intangible spirit been born? Perhaps all three. Perhaps none. Perhaps it is foolish to search (*Pause.*) for answers.

*He is once again enveloped in mist.*

*The College Administration Building.* **Fielding** *and* **Adela**.

**Adela** Thank you for giving me refuge.

**Fielding** I had to take you out of that crowd.

**Adela** Have you any explanation of my extraordinary behaviour?

**Fielding** Have I? None. Why make a charge if you were going to withdraw it?

**Adela** Why indeed?

**Fielding** I ought to feel grateful to you, I suppose, but –

**Adela** I don't expect gratitude. (*Pause.*) My echo is gone. I call the buzzing sound in my ears an echo. I have been unwell ever since that expedition to the caves, and possibly before it.

**Fielding** What kind of illness?

**Adela** *touches her head at the side, then shakes it.*

**Fielding** That was my first thought, the day of the arrest: hallucination.

**Adela** Do you think that could be so?

**Fielding** Can you remember when you first felt out of sorts?

**Adela** When I came to tea with you here, I enjoyed the singing . . . but just about then a sort of sadness began that I couldn't detect at the time . . . no, nothing as solid as sadness. Living at half-pressure expresses it best. Various

other things happened – it doesn't matter what, but I was
under par for all of them. I was certainly in that state when I
saw the caves, and it is possible I had a hallucination there,
the sort of thing – though in an awful form – that makes
some women think they've had an offer of marriage when
none was made.

**Fielding**   You put it honestly, anyhow.

**Adela**   I was brought up to be honest; the trouble is it gets
me nowhere.

**Fielding**   It'll get us to heaven.

**Adela**   Will it?

**Fielding**   If heaven exists.

**Hamidullah** *enters and is very distressed to see* **Adela**.

**Hamidullah**   Hello, my dear Fielding. We are all
celebrating. Aziz is waiting. Can you join us?

**Fielding**   At once?

**Adela**   I hope to leave in a moment, don't let me
interrupt.

**Fielding**   The telephone lines are broken – cut, actually.
Miss Quested can't ring up her friends.

**Hamidullah**   A great deal has been broken; more than
will ever be mended. Still, there should be some way of
transporting this lady back to Civil Lines.

**Adela**   I shall go to the Dak bungalow.

**Fielding**   I have a better idea than that, Miss Quested.
You must stop here at the college. I shall be away at least
two days, and you can have the place entirely to yourself.

**Hamidullah**   I don't agree at all. There might be another
demonstration tonight and suppose an attack is made on the
college. You would be held responsible for this lady's safety,
my dear fellow.

**Fielding**   They might equally attack the Dak bungalow.

**Hamidullah**   Exactly. But the responsibility ceases to be yours.

**Fielding**   She is not going to the Dak bungalow.

**Hamidullah**   Then where is she to go? *We shall never have done with her!*

**Adela**   I understand that I offend you . . .

**Hamidullah**   You do not appeal to me, Miss Quested. If you had shown emotion in court, if you had broken down, if you had beaten your breast and invoked the name of God, you might have touched my imagination and generosity. But you exhibited no passion or love for those you had wronged. Truth is not truth unless it is accompanied by kindness. And more kindness. I reject your sacrifice because, though it came from your heart, it did not include your heart. (**Adela** *is stricken by his words; he looks out at the veranda.*) Well, anyway, here is our solution. Here comes the City Magistrate.

**Adela**   At last! Will you ask him what he wants, Mr Fielding?

**Fielding**   He wants you, of course.

**Adela**   He may not even know I'm here.

**Fielding**   I'll see him first, if you prefer. (**Fielding** *walks on to the veranda.*)

**Hamidullah**   Really – need you have exposed Fielding to this further discomfort? He is far too considerate.

*There is complete silence between them.* **Fielding** *returns.*

**Fielding**   He has some news for you. You'll find him on the veranda. He prefers not to come in.

**Adela**   Yes. (*Pause.*) You have been wonderfully kind to me. (*Goes out to the veranda.*)

**Fielding**   He has had a cable to the effect that his mother's dead.

**Hamidullah**   Oh, really, Mrs Moore. I'm sorry.

**Fielding**   She died on her journey.

**Hamidullah**   The heat, I suppose.

**Fielding**   Let us not mention this to Aziz this evening, not on his happy night. He loved her.

**Adela** *returns.*

**Hamidullah**   Oh, this is unbearable!

**Adela** (*sits*)   Ah, me!

**Fielding**   Heaslop is waiting for you, I think.

**Adela**   I do so long to be alone. She was my best friend, far more to me than him. I can't bear to be with Ronny. Could you do me the very great kindness of letting me stop after all?

**Hamidullah**   Bloody hell.

*A light on* **Adela** *– sitting in a chair at the College Administration Building, slowly drinking a glass of water.*

*On the other side of the stage – a rooftop. The* **Revellers** *are lying around, under mosquito nets, looking at the stars and trying to come down after an evening of drink and the pipe.* **Aziz** *and* **Fielding** *lie next to each other,* **Fielding** *in native dress.*

**Fielding**   Aziz, are you awake?

**Aziz**   No, so let us have a talk. Is this not a perfect end to our celebration?

**Fielding**   Perfect. Look at the stars.

**Aziz**   Let us dream plans for the future.

**Fielding**   I am useless at dreaming.

**Aziz**    Then goodnight. (*Turns away.*) Are you content with our day's work, Cyril?

**Fielding**    Are you?

**Aziz** (*turns back*)    Except that I ate too much. And drank too much probably. But I do want to plan. We can spend our holidays together, can't we? Visit Kashmir, possibly Persia. I shall have plenty of money. Miss Quested will have to pay me at least twenty thousand rupees as compensation. While with me you shall never spend a single pie. This is what I have always wanted, and as a result of my misfortunes, it has come.

**Adela** *pours herself another glass of water.*

**Fielding**    You have won a great victory –

**Aziz**    Ah. I know what you are going to say next. Let Miss Quested off paying. Am I not right? I can sense it in your voice.

**Fielding**    I *was* thinking that.

**Aziz**    So then the English may say, 'Here is a native who has actually behaved like a gentleman.'

**Fielding**    My dear fellow, I quite agree, she must pay all your costs, that is only fair, but do not treat her like a conquered enemy. The sum you mentioned would ruin her.

**Aziz**    You really do think that by letting Miss Quested off easily I shall make a better reputation for myself and Indians generally. No, no, it will be put down to weakness and the attempt to gain promotion officially. I have decided to have nothing more to do with British India, as a matter of fact. I shall seek service in some independent state.

**Adela** *slowly drinks the water.*

**Fielding**    In the course of a conversation with Miss Quested . . .

**Aziz**    I don't want to hear.

**Fielding**  Be quiet – in the course of a conversation with
Miss Quested I have begun to understand her character.
She is a prig, as I have always said, but she is perfectly
genuine and very brave. When she saw she was wrong, she
said so. In doing so, she destroyed her standing and her
reputation among her compatriots. Do treat her
considerately. She really mustn't get the worst of both
worlds.

**Adela** *pours water on a cloth and presses it against her forehead.*

**Aziz**  Not even Mogul emperors showed mercy until they
received an apology.

**Fielding**  She'll apologise if that's the problem. Look, I'll
make you an offer. Dictate to me whatever form of words
you like, and this time tomorrow I'll bring it back signed.

**Aziz**  'Dear Dr Aziz, I wish you had come into the cave; I
am an awful old hag, and it is my last chance.' Will she sign
that?

**Adela** *spills the pitcher of water. She turns her face away.*

**Fielding**  Well, goodnight, goodnight, it's time to go to
sleep after that.

**Aziz**  Goodnight, I suppose it is. (*Pause.*) I have an idea
which will satisfy your tender mind. I shall consult Mrs
Moore. Her opinion will solve everything; I can trust her so
absolutely.

**Fielding**  You are so fantastic . . . Miss Quested you won't
treat generously, despite the fact that she behaved decently
this morning; while over Mrs Moore there is this elaborate
chivalry whereas the old lady never did anything for you at
all.

**Aziz**  I have seen her but three times, but I know she is an
Oriental.

**Fielding**  Ah. Then you know what Mrs Moore would tell
you. In your heart, Aziz, you know exactly what she would

say. She would want you to spare the woman who was about to marry her son.

**Aziz** (*pause*)    Indeed. (*Pause.*) Then I will spare her. (*Pause.*) I think Cyril Fielding is a very nice chap and my best friend, but in some ways a fool. (*He turns away and closes his eyes.*)

**Adela** *closes her eyes.*

**Godbole** *on the carpet. A procession is forming. His* **Students** *have taken up instruments. They play a melody.*

**Godbole**    We gather now to prepare our ceremony. Has our God heard the melody? Perhaps. But is our song even meant for our God? And where is God Himself, in whose honour this congregation has gathered? Smothered under rose leaves, overhung by oleographs, entirely obscured, when the wind blows, by the tattered foilage of a banana. His face cannot be seen. And the inscriptions, which the poets of the state have composed, are hung high – high – where they cannot be read.

*The Government College.* **Fielding** *and* **Adela**.

**Adela**    I am returning to England. Ronny has broken our engagement. Far wiser of him. I ought to have spoken myself, but I drifted on, wondering what would happen. I would willingly have gone on spoiling his life through inertia. Oh, the trouble I've brought on everyone here . . . I can never get over it. We ought never to have thought of marriage.

**Fielding**    About marriage I am cynical.

**Adela**    I am not. This false start has been all my own fault. I entered that cave thinking 'Am I fond of him?' Tenderness, respect . . . I tried to make them take the place of . . .

**Fielding**    I no longer want love.

**Adela**    No more do I. But I want others to want it. (*Pause.*) We will meet again, I hope.

**Fielding**   We will, in England, if I take home leave, which, as a matter of fact, might happen shortly.

**Adela**   Oh, that would be very nice. (*She smiles.*)

**Aziz** *and* **Fielding** *at dinner.*

**Fielding**   I am going quite soon to England. I am only going for a little time. On official business.

**Adela** – *on the other side of the stage – stands by the railings on the deck of a ship, watching the water.*

**Aziz**   Will your business leave you much spare time?

**Fielding**   Enough to see my friends.

**Aziz**   Will you see Miss Quested?

**Fielding**   If I have time.

**Aziz**   I imagine you'll enjoy that.

**Fielding**   You have a peculiar tone of voice.

**Aziz**   I suppose you know there is gossip about you. They say that you and Miss Quested became rather too intimate friends after the trial, that you and she have been guilty of impropriety.

**Fielding**   They would say that.

**Aziz**   It's all over the town and may injure your reputation. I have tried all I could to silence such a story. Even though . . .

**Fielding**   What?

**Aziz**   There is perhaps some truth in it? Perhaps you and Mademoiselle Adela used to amuse one another in the evening, naughty boy.

**Fielding**   You little rotter! Well, I'm damned. Amusement indeed. Is it likely at such a time?

**Aziz**   Oh, I beg your pardon, I'm sure. The licentious oriental imagination was at work.

**Fielding**   You see, Aziz: the circumstances . . . also the girl was still engaged to Heaslop, also I never felt . . .

**Aziz**   Yes, yes . . . your little rotter was out of line.

**Fielding**   I've offended you.

**Aziz**   Most certainly you have not.

**Fielding**   I was unintentionally rude. Unreserved regrets.

**Aziz**   It is nothing, we all of us make mistakes. In a friendship such as ours a few slips are of no consequence. Shall we talk about something else?

**Fielding**   What subject?

**Aziz**   Poetry. Let us discuss why poetry has lost the power of making men brave. My mother's father was also a poet and fought against you in the mutiny. As it is, I am a doctor, who has won a case and has three children to support. I am, I suppose, what is known as a mature man. When you knew me first, I was a child. Everyone was my friend then. The Friend: a Persian expression for God.

**Aziz** *looks at* **Fielding** *and then looks away.*

**Adela** *takes out a letter and reads it. A sea wind blows her hair.*

*A shrine next to a tree. Messages are scrawled. Flowers and earthenware saucers laid as gifts. Several* **Indians** *bow in front of the shrine and leave other offerings. They then move away.* **Ronny** *and* **Turton** *move out of the shadows.*

**Ronny**   I'll be damned . . .

**Turton**   It's the start of a cult, I'm afraid. (*Picks up a bouquet of flowers.*) Esmiss Esmoor . . .

**Ronny**   She's still giving trouble, still mixing herself up with natives . . .

**Turton**   It isn't her fault, dear boy, after all she's . . .

**Ronny**   Dead? What does happen to one's mother when she dies, I wonder? Presumably she goes to heaven.

Anyhow, she clears out. (*Looks at flowers.*) Usually she doesn't become a minor god.

**Turton**    I think after a few months it might die down.

**Adela** *folds the letter and puts it in her pocket. She leaves the ship's deck.*

*She is enveloped in fog and disappears.*

**Worshippers** *sing a mantra.*

**Worshippers**    Esmiss Esmoor, Esmiss Esmoor . . . (*And then they too are enveloped by the fog.*)

*A cobra – a live version of the papier-mâché cobra – jumps out of the mist and disappears.*

*Mau* **Villagers** *carry the wooden cradle aloft on the altar, followed by the* **Students** *who are enacting the* **Band of Sweepers** *and then they too disappear.*

*The mist evaporates. Mau.* **Aziz** *stands in the garden by the Shrine of the Body, staring at* **Fielding** *and* **Boy**.

**Aziz**    I have forgotten all of you. You no longer exist. (*Starts to leave.*)

**Fielding**    I understand there's an interesting procession from the water this evening.

**Aziz**    I wouldn't know.

**Fielding**    Do you think they would object to English people watching the procession?

**Aziz**    I know nothing at all about the religion here. Mau is a Hindu state.

**Fielding**    We had a very different reception both at Mudkul and Deora; they were kindness itself at Deora.

**Aziz**    You should never have left them.

**Fielding**    Indeed. Come, Ralph. (*Takes the* **Boy** *by the shoulder and starts to lead him away.*)

**Aziz**    Goodbye, Mr Fielding, goodbye, Mr Quested.

**Fielding**    Who on earth is Mr Quested?

**Aziz**    Do I mispronounce that well-known name? Is this not your wife's brother?

**Fielding**    Who on earth do you suppose I've married?

**Boy**    I'm only Ralph Moore.

**Fielding**    Don't you know that my wife was Mrs Moore's daughter?

**Aziz** *blanches, then looks away.*

**Fielding**    Perhaps this explains your odd attitude.

**Aziz**    What is wrong with my attitude?

**Fielding**    Your refusal to answer any of my letters.

**Aziz**    This is a very useless conversation.

**Fielding**    How did you ever make such a mistake? I should think I wrote you half a dozen times, mentioning my wife by name. Miss Quested? Miss Quested is our friend, she introduced us, but . . .

**Aziz**    So there. It amounts to the same thing. You are Heaslop's brother-in-law, are you not? What does it matter to me whom you marry? Yes, yes, I made a foolish blunder. You wrote that you had married, I read no further, I had no need to. I thought you married my enemy. I thought you'd stolen my money, but it's *as if* you stole it. (*Pause.*) I read no further. (**Aziz** *walks off.*)

**Godbole** *on the carpet, as a statue of the God is loaded on to a litter. His* **Students** *are with him, as are some* **Villagers**.

**Godbole**    The procession is about to begin. It is said that saints are made in the image of gods, but perhaps it is the other way round. Has not our God learned something from our local saint, he of the separated head and body? And so

tonight in his honour, we will march to the prison and
release a prisoner.

**Aziz** *enters.*

**Aziz**    I have seen Fielding.

**Godbole**    Excellent.

**Aziz**    He has not married Miss Quested.

**Godbole**    Ah no, he married the sister of Mr Heaslop. Ah,
exactly. I have known that for over a year.

**Aziz**    Why did you not tell me?

**Godbole**    Did I not?

**Aziz**    Your silence plunged me into a pretty pickle.

**Godbole**    Never be angry with me. I am, as far as my
limitations permit, your true friend. Besides, it is my holy
festival.

**Aziz** *nods and walks away.*

**Godbole**    Noise. (*Pause.*) Noise, incense on the altar,
sweat, the blaze of lights, wind in the bananas, noise,
thunder. Our God is born. At last, the ceremony has begun.
The procession begins . . .

**Godbole** *dances down a pathway along with his* **Students***, and
the statue, and the napkin, as they lead a procession to the prison.*

*The Government Guest House.* **Aziz** *walks in and finds* **Ralph***.*

**Aziz**    How are the celebrated bee-stings?

**Ralph**    They throb rather.

**Aziz**    Come here, please. Allow me to look.

**Ralph** *goes to* **Aziz***.* **Aziz** *studies his wrist.*

**Aziz**    I have brought you some salve.

**Ralph**    Please leave it with me. Your hands are unkind.

**Aziz**   Certainly not. Now, do you want me to treat your
stings or do you prefer an English doctor? There is one at
Asirgarh, about fifty miles away. I think I had better see Mr
Fielding about you; this is really great nonsense, your
present behaviour.

**Ralph**   You should not treat us like this . . .

**Aziz**   Like what?

**Ralph**   Dr Aziz, we have done you no harm.

**Aziz**   Aha, you know my name, I see. Yes, I am Aziz. No,
of course your great friend Miss Quested did me no harm at
the Marabar.

*All the guns of the state go off in the near distance. A rocket is released
in the sky. The whole town has become a blur of light.*

**Ralph**   What is happening?

**Aziz**   The procession has reached the prison. Each year
they release one prisoner to satisfy the God. It is the only
part of their ritual that I know or understand. (*Pause.*) I too
was a prisoner.

*Sounds of the* **Singers** *and the* **Band** *fill the night air.*

**Singers** (*in the distance*)
    Radhakrishna, Radhakrishna,
    Radhakrishna, Radhakrishna,
    Krishnaradha, Krishnaradha,
    Radhakrishna, Radhakrishna . . .

**Aziz**   I must go back now, goodnight . . . (*Holds out his hand,
which* **Ralph** *takes.*) Don't you think me unkind any more?

**Ralph**   No.

**Aziz**   How can you tell, you strange fellow?

**Ralph**   Not difficult, the one thing I always know.

**Aziz**   Can you always tell whether a stranger is your
friend?

**Ralph**   Yes.

**Aziz**   Then you are an Oriental. (*He hands the ointment to* **Ralph**.) Take this, think of me when you use it. I shall never want it back. I must give you one little present, and it is all I have got; you are Mrs Moore's son.

**Ralph**   I am that.

**Aziz**   Did your mother speak to you about me?

**Ralph**   In her letters, in her letter. She loved you.

**Aziz**   Yes, your mother was my best friend in all the world.

*A wind begins to rise.*

Soon it will be our monsoon, our best weather. How I wish she could have seen them, the rains. Now is the time when all things are happy, young and old. This is India. (*He smiles.*)

**Godbole**, *again on the strip of carpet, addresses the audience. The* **Students** *and the procession stand behind him.*

**Godbole**   The prisoner has been released and so, too, has been something unknowable in our spirit. Later, much later, we will take the statue of the God – the napkin, the cradle – down to the water's edge, and we will throw God away. Throw God Himself into the storm. Thus He is thrown year after year, an emblem of passage, a passage not easy, not now, not here, not to be apprehended except when it is unattainable. And then the ceremony shall be over. They will take down the banners. They will take down GOD SI LOVE. And so, finally, what will it have been about, the ceremony of the God? Do you wish to know its meaning? Can you say where was the emotional centre of it – the core, so to speak? I think you cannot. How can you locate the heart of a cloud? (*Pause.*) I am – myself – most inadequate. I have said to the God, Come, come, come . . . At the same time I have tried to place myself in the position of the God and to love whomever my mind touches upon. (*Pause.*) Like that old woman. (*Pause.*) Like that wasp.

*The music starts again. The* **Band** *plays. The* **Singers** *sing. They dance.* **Godbole** *joins them, dancing. Then suddenly it seems that he is dancing with* **Mrs Moore***. They seem to float above the town, and then they all – all – disappear.*

**Aziz** *and* **Fielding** *sit in a field.*

**Fielding**    We leave in the morning.

**Aziz**    I know.

*Silence.*

Was your trip a success?

**Fielding**    I think not. The schools I have inspected have been most inadequate. Compared to our school in Chandrapore, certainly.

**Aziz** *looks at him, is about to comment, doesn't. A pause.*

**Aziz**    I have written to Miss Quested. Thanking her for her fine behaviour two years back. It is perfectly plain to me now that she behaved well. I thought how brave she was and decided to tell her so. And I promised my children would speak of her with the greatest affection and respect.

**Fielding**    She will be greatly pleased.

**Aziz**    I want to do kind actions all round and wipe out the wretched business of Marabar for ever. I have been so foolish, thinking you meant to get hold of my money; as bad a mistake as the cave itself.

**Fielding**    I wish you would talk to my wife. She too believes that Marabar is wiped out.

**Aziz**    How so?

**Fielding**    I don't know. Perhaps she will tell you. She won't tell me. My wife is after something. You and I are, roughly speaking, not after anything. We jog on as decently as we can, you a little in front. But my wife is not with us. Nor is her brother. They both suffer from restlessness. Not unlike their mother. They found something soothing here –

this Krishna business perhaps. They won't talk to me about this. They know I think a certain side of their lives is a mistake. That's why I wish you would talk to her.

**Aziz**   No. I will not.

**Fielding**   But why?

**Aziz**   I might like her. (*Pause.*) Let's not spoil our last few minutes together.

**Fielding**   Surely we shall see each other again.

**Aziz**   I think not. I want you to clear out – all of you, you too. Even you. You and the Turtons and the Callenders and the Miss Dereks. Even you. My dear Cyril, you found our schools a disgrace because deep inside you think that we Indians can't do anything right without you. We go to seed without you. Yes, even you think that. No – clear out, clear out, I say. Why are we put to so much suffering? We used to blame you, now we blame ourselves, we grow wiser. Until England is in difficulties we keep silent, but in the next European war – aha, aha! Then is our time.

**Fielding**   Whom do you want instead of the English? The Japanese?

**Aziz**   No, the Afghans. My own ancestors.

**Fielding**   Oh, your Hindu friends will like that, won't they?

**Aziz**   It will be arranged – a conference of oriental statesmen. India shall be a nation. No foreigners of any sort! Hindu and Moslem and Sikh and all shall be one! Hurrah! Hurrah for India!

**Fielding**   India a nation! Taking your seat with Guatemala and Belgium, I suppose.

**Aziz** (*rises, agitated*)   Clear out, you fellows, double quick, I say. We may hate one another, but we hate you most. If I don't make you go, my children will. If it's fifty or five hundred years we shall get rid of you, yes, we shall drive every blasted Englishman into the sea, and then . . . (*Half kisses him.*) And then you and I shall be friends.

**Aziz** *walks away.*

**Fielding**   Why can't we be friends now? It's what I want. It's what you want.

**Aziz** *looks at him, then shakes his head.*

**Aziz**   No. Not yet.

**Aziz** *leaves.*

**Fielding** *looks after him, then walks away.*

*Only the Shrines of the Head and Body remain.*

# Methuen Contemporary Dramatists
*include*

Peter Barnes (three volumes)
Sebastian Barry
Edward Bond (six volumes)
Howard Brenton
 (two volumes)
Richard Cameron
Jim Cartwright
Caryl Churchill (two volumes)
Sarah Daniels (two volumes)
Nick Darke
David Edgar (three volumes)
Ben Elton
Dario Fo (two volumes)
Michael Frayn (two volumes)
Paul Godfrey
John Guare
Peter Handke
Jonathan Harvey
Declan Hughes
Terry Johnson (two volumes)
Bernard-Marie Koltès
David Lan
Bryony Lavery
Doug Lucie
David Mamet (three volumes)

Martin McDonagh
Duncan McLean
Anthony Minghella
 (two volumes)
Tom Murphy (four volumes)
Phyllis Nagy
Anthony Nielsen
Philip Osment
Louise Page
Joe Penhall
Stephen Poliakoff
 (three volumes)
Christina Reid
Philip Ridley
Willy Russell
Ntozake Shange
Sam Shepard (two volumes)
Wole Soyinka (two volumes)
David Storey (three volumes)
Sue Townsend
Michel Vinaver (two volumes)
Michael Wilcox
David Wood (two volumes)
Victoria Wood

# Methuen World Classics

*include*

Jean Anouilh (two volumes)
John Arden (two volumes)
Arden & D'Arcy
Brendan Behan
Aphra Behn
Bertolt Brecht (six volumes)
Büchner
Bulgakov
Calderón
Čapek
Anton Chekhov
Noël Coward (seven volumes)
Eduardo De Filippo
Max Frisch
John Galsworthy
Gogol
Gorky
Harley Granville Barker
    (two volumes)
Henrik Ibsen (six volumes)
Lorca (three volumes)

Marivaux
Mustapha Matura
David Mercer (two volumes)
Arthur Miller (five volumes)
Molière
Musset
Peter Nichols (two volumes)
Clifford Odets
Joe Orton
A. W. Pinero
Luigi Pirandello
Terence Rattigan
    (two volumes)
W. Somerset Maughan
    (two volumes)
August Strindberg
    (three volumes)
J. M. Synge
Ramón del Valle-Inclán
Frank Wedekind
Oscar Wilde

# Methuen Modern Plays

*include work by*

Jean Anouilh
John Arden
Margaretta D'Arcy
Peter Barnes
Sebastian Barry
Brendan Behan
Dermot Bolger
Edward Bond
Bertolt Brecht
Howard Brenton
Anthony Burgess
Simon Burke
Jim Cartwright
Caryl Churchill
Noël Coward
Lucinda Coxon
Sarah Daniels
Nick Darke
Nick Dear
Shelagh Delaney
David Edgar
David Eldridge
Dario Fo
Michael Frayn
John Godber
Paul Godfrey
David Greig
John Guare
Peter Handke
David Harrower
Jonathan Harvey
Iain Heggie
Declan Hughes
Terry Johnson
Sarah Kane
Charlotte Keatley
Barrie Keeffe
Howard Korder

Robert Lepage
Stephen Lowe
Doug Lucie
Martin McDonagh
John McGrath
Terrence McNally
David Mamet
Patrick Marber
Arthur Miller
Mtwa, Ngema & Simon
Tom Murphy
Phyllis Nagy
Peter Nichols
Joseph O'Connor
Joe Orton
Louise Page
Joe Penhall
Luigi Pirandello
Stephen Poliakoff
Franca Rame
Mark Ravenhill
Philip Ridley
Reginald Rose
David Rudkin
Willy Russell
Jean-Paul Sartre
Sam Shepard
Wole Soyinka
Shelagh Stephenson
C. P. Taylor
Theatre de Complicite
Theatre Workshop
Sue Townsend
Judy Upton
Timberlake Wertenbaker
Roy Williams
Victoria Wood

For a complete catalogue of Methuen Drama titles
write to:

Methuen Drama
215 Vauxhall Bridge Road
London SW1V 1EJ

or you can visit our website at:

www.methuen.co.uk